Endeared
by Dark

The Porcupine's Quill

CANADIAN CATALOGUING IN PUBLICATION DATA

Johnston, George, 1913 Oct. 7-
 Endeared by dark

ISBN 0-88984-107-1

I. Title.

PS8519.0437A17 1990   C811'.54   C90-094064-6
PR9199.3.J6A17 1990

Second printing 1991.

The poems 'War on the Periphery', 'Rapture', 'Roses', 'O
Earth, Turn!' and 'Ice at Last' are copyright The New Yorker
Magazine, Inc.

Published by The Porcupine's Quill, Inc., 68 Main Street,
Erin, Ontario NOB 1TO with financial assistance from the
Canada Council and the Ontario Arts Council.

Distributed by The University of Toronto Press,
5201 Dufferin Street, Downsview, Ontario M5H 5T8.

Readied for the press by John Metcalf.

The cover is after a drawing by Virgil Burnett based on a
photograph of the prow of the Oseberg ship (c. 800) discovered
near Oslo in 1903.

Printed and bound by The Porcupine's Quill, Inc.
The stock is Zephyr laid, and the type, Ehrhardt.

Endeared by Dark

for Lallie & Maxwell
with love
from George & Jeanne.
December 3 1993

George Johnston

The Collected Poems

for Mark

WILL THE POEMS that one has made, in answer to some deep-seated prompting, find readers in the big world and stay with them for a while? Of the thousand thousand pages of verse that are published and recited, only a few will do this, and who knows which ones, or what about them will make them remembered?

Verse came before prose, and kept in mind what wanted to be kept in times before writing had become common. Stored records have taken over from memory, and prose rhythms have encroached on the title of verse, and now remembered poetry speaks to a corner of the imagination that only a few of us still tend. It speaks to the child in us, and the sage too.

Poetic lines will stay with us, whether we understand what they mean or not. Their rhythms are homely as breathing, heartbeat, autumnal insect noises, the wash of sea on shore:

> Come unto these yellow sands,
>   And then take hands:
> Curtsied when you have and kiss'd
>   The wild waves whist ...

The meaning need hardly be understood, since the lines are held in the memory. If a full understanding does not come, the form may be enough by itself. Many kinds of poetic meaning come second: rhythm, and then a familiarity that goes deeper than understanding.

Prose has its rhythms and meanings, and these too are knit together and so move us, but prose feels a responsibility to persuasion, and its rhythms are not poetic. Repetitive rhythms in prose become distressing, they seem to take on airs, whereas repetition is in the grain of poetry.

Rhyme, in its many forms, will make speech memorable. Rhyme is a happy achievement; it has the happiness of luck, and however hard the finding of it may have been, it has a sweet element of the given. It calls for instinct as well as drudgery and discipline, for a proper rhyme must make company with the sounds that go before and come after it, and it must be at home in its logical surroundings. Dictionaries may be helpful in rhyming, and indeed in many ways, especially those that give representation of historical usage: in English this means above all the great Oxford Dictionary, the OED, the 'majestic object' as William Empson calls it. Rhymes, however, are best hunted in memory, whose ways are footpaths that lead through turns of meaning not otherwise come upon. Half rhymes have their graces too, though these seem most satisfactory when the consonants rhyme true. Consonants hardly change over the centuries; vowel sounds are fickle.

The commonness of rhyme, by which it is at home in doggerel, and not just in lyric and elegy, is a mark of its humanity, and this makes the distaste for it, which many now express, seem a kind of snobbery. Though fine poets continue to compose in them, rhymed and measured forms have lately been scorned by others, who would persuade us that they are out of fashion. Rhyme and metre, in their varieties, have been formative in English verse for as long as we know of such a thing. Now we are told that they have been left behind, because a corner has been turned, and there is no looking back; verse, it is said, has been freed from the older conventions of form. In effect, this has reduced much of it to a sameness and monotony of rhythm, however artfully the lines are begun and ended and spaced about. Moreover, its new freedom has all but shut out the common reader. Poets now look for response from fellow poets. The common reader of poetry, who not long ago would have had by heart Gray's *Elegy*, or Pope's *Essay on Man*, or some Wordsworth or Browning or Tennyson, is given little to remember. Not themselves poets, they are generous lovers of poetry, and their numbers are dwindling. Every poet hopes for a few; the least sign from them is heartening. They do not ask to be written down to, any more than children do, but they are most likely to be invited by the pleasures of rememberable poetry, as children naturally are. Many nursery rhymes, now looked on as especially of the child's world, were once adult poems. Some were political. Children take readily to rhythm and rhyme, and they will give poetry a strong beat when they read it out, often regardless of sense; some adults will do the same. What is the point in discouraging this? Let the sense come in its time. Poetry as such may be our worst taught subject. How can there be examinations in it? Are its rhythms ever taught? How can poetry be taught or the reading of it encouraged without acknowledging the importance of its rhythms?

This leads to a query about creative writing. The word 'creative' to begin with is a puzzle. Whether they believe in a creation or not, poets, like all other artists, must make from what they have been given and what they can find. Aside from the question of creation, how is writing to be taught? Artists of every kind need and seek instruction in their proper mediums. They must know life, by whatever means, but that is not the medium for any art. There is a sense in which life itself has been considered an art, but setting that aside, what do artists want to know? Painters learn about colours, vehicles, proportions, brushes, the history of painting and so on. Every art, whether of making or performing, demands a knowledge of its medium and history. Of poetry the medium is language, and to know it one must know its grammar, syntax, diction and history. If a creative writing course were to offer a study of these four how many students would it attract? How many instructors would undertake to teach them? Would public funds be found for such a course? Poets have become shy of learning about their medium as they never have been before. Lady Bracknell anticipated this new feeling for purity. I do not approve of anything that tampers with natural ignorance, she says. Ignorance is like a delicate exotic fruit; touch it and the bloom is gone.

The teaching of grammar and syntax has been associated with correctness, a concern few contemporary poets are likely to feel. English grammar, syntax and diction, however, do not concern correctness but usage; they are properly studied historically, to learn how the language works and has worked, and to find out the ways of this most wayward of mediums. Again, its comprehensive handbook is the great Oxford Dictionary. Correctness has not been a foible of English styles, in prose or poetry, and the great eighteenth-century writers were not so attached to it as they pretended to be. A close look at sentences from Addison, Steele, Swift or Hume, who wrote with grace and energy, will reveal hazardous constructions and syntactical long chances. Many of Pope's couplets are balancing turns that seem to be poised on slight syntactical pivots:

> 'Tis sung, when Midas' Ears began to spring,
> (Midas, a sacred person and a King)
> His very Minister who spy'd them first,
> (Some say his Queen) was forc'd to speak or burst.

The urbanity of the rhythm is worth noting as well, and the strong groundswell rhythm that underlies it.

The current suspicion of grammar seems to spring from deep sources, perhaps from despair of the language itself. A poet may wonder if English any longer exists. It is full of distractions and temptations: slang, current catch phrases and specialized jargons in one's local form of it, and in its midst, introduced by print, radio and television, other local forms, with their exotic, and perhaps ephemeral, ways of saying things. Where does one turn for an English that may be worked into a lasting fabric?

A great poet of our recent past, C.M. Doughty, looked to pre-Shakespearian English for his words, especially to the poetry of Chaucer and Spenser. Such an English need not be archaic; a full working vocabulary of it is still at hand in everyday speech and may be found by clearing away current ephemera and the jargons of debased scientific and technological coinages. It is not a pure language, English has not been that since well before Chaucer, but it is a faithful language for poetry, and it includes earlier Latin and Greek borrowings that in some contexts will add a gorgeousness or a fine mock-heroic effect. David Jones, for example, weighs his English and makes use of its borrowings with discernment; his very choice of words is poetry. Shakespeare and Milton were cunning in their use of borrowings. Shakespeare would be rhetorical in Latin and then translate his rhetoric into English, as for example when Macbeth, after the murder of Duncan, asks whether all great Neptune's ocean will wash his hand clean:

> No, this my hand will rather
> The multitudinous seas incarnadine
> Making the green one red.

Multitudinous and incarnadine may be Shakespeare's own borrowings; at any rate, his are the earliest entries for these words in the OED. Doughty would no doubt have rejected them, and Shakespeare himself kept the English of his songs pure of such Latinate words, and also many lyrical passages of dialogue, for example Lorenzo's speech to Jessica that begins, How sweet the moonlight sleeps upon this bank. Such purity of diction may again be found in Blake's *Songs of Innocence and Experience,* and to come close to home, in Jay Macpherson's *The Boatman,* a book all its own in modern English poetry, and one of the more simply beautiful.

Such poetry is marked by the now rarely-sought virtue of anonymity, which is common to the world's great poetry of the past, and to much indeed that bears a maker's name. Poetry that survives in memory will become anonymous. Though it may be strong in personal feeling, it expresses nothing so much as poetry itself. Verse composition is now thought to be a form of self-expression; sometimes it is said to be therapy. Critics give a poem the poet's name: Noakes is or Noakes says or Noakes argues here or takes a stand there. Poets have their photographs on their books, and they give public readings of their poems, seldom for the pleasure of sounding their rhythmic patterns or chanting them, but more often for a kind of audience response that they call feedback. Few poets, if any, are untouched by this, and small wonder: the rewards for writing verse, whether it is poetry or not, are few. Money rewards are scarce and recognition, sweet as it is, can never be enough; the whole world will not satisfy a craving for it. Nor need verse be expected to further a cause; nothing could be less trustworthy. Verse with a message that does find readers will mean what it chooses to mean, often in contempt of its intended sense.

The rewards for the making of verse come in the doing of it, doing it not just well but superlatively well – an illusion, probably – and then, for a short while after, in the feeling that one has perhaps done it. Blake sang his songs to his own tunes, and copied them out and decorated them. A maker may guess that the thing is poetry and yet be sure that the last answer about this is something that no one can give. Moreover, poetry or not, it will have meanings and feelings of its own, and if it is well made and becomes well read and remembered by many or a few, it will free itself of its maker and live its own life, perhaps short, perhaps very long. The same may be said of a body of verse: once published it will be on its own and may or may not acknowledge its maker again.

Poetry is where one finds it. Of all the lines of verse published, if one can bear to think of their multitude, only a few may be considered poetry. Of the rest, some may be witty or seductive or beautiful or horrifying, impressive in many ways and admirable, and yet not poetry. A.E. Housman, in *The Name and Nature of Poetry*, says, 'If a man is insensible to poetry, it does not follow that he gets no pleasure from poems. Poems very seldom consist of poetry and nothing else; and pleasure can be derived also from their other ingredients.' Poetry comes very much in the how of it, in its rhythms most surely, in the handling of its sounds, whether smooth or harsh, in its word choice and phrasing and in something else, seldom mentioned but perhaps most important, in the physical effect of its syllables. Who better than Housman has written of the physical effect of reading, or thinking of poetry? The framing of certain word combinations in the throat and head passages when reading silently as well as aloud will bring a tightening of the throat and tears to the eyes, marks of the presence of poetry, he says:

> And wild and high the *Cameron's Gathering* rose!
> The war-note of Lochiel, which Albyn's hills
> Have heard ...

These syllables in the emotional press of their context can hardly be read without a break in the voice, and yet a small part of this reaction, a triggering effect, may be the very feeling of the syllables 'wild' and 'high' in one's throat.

Canadian poetry is well supplied with other ingredients, some of a high order of excellence: wit, true sentiment, clarity, passion and justness of observation, all the admirable 'what' of poetry. Our critics have much to say about these, but for the all-important 'how' they have hardly a word, unless perhaps the meaningless 'crafted' or 'honed'. No doubt the 'how' is there in our poetry, if we will learn to read for it.

THE POOL

A boy gazing in a pool
Is all profound; his eyes are cool
And he's as though unborn, he's gone;
He's the abyss he gazes on.

A man searches the pool in vain
For his profundity again;
He finds it neither there nor here
And all between is pride and fear.

His eyes are warm with love and death,
Time makes a measure of his breath;
The world is now profound and he
Fearful, on its periphery.

LOVE OF THE CITY

After a week of wandering through the world,
Eating wherever we could, sleeping, washing ourselves
Wherever we could, in bars and railway rooms,
We came to this great city. Nothing
Will persuade us ever to leave it again.

The city loves us now it's moved us in:
The yellow sky comes down and fills the room;
Dirt on the floor is kind, the walls are kind,
Everyone's kind to us wherever we go.

And truly, when death comes, where will he find
A better room than here, better arrangements,
More courtesy, more eager friendliness
Than in this excellent street-scattered city,
This home, this network, this great roof of pity?

MOONLIGHT

Those of us who love the moon
   And pause to look at her
Turn our protected souls too soon
   Out of her naked air.

Yet up she comes across the sky
   Lenticular and still
Putting the secret darkness by
   On floor and window sill.

How does she look on us who now
   Leave her explicit light
Turning, with angel-guarded brow,
   Each to his private night?

NIGHT NOISES

Late at night in night's neglected places
The busy diesel shunter thumps and grinds
As to and fro he singles out and chases
The helpless cars, whose businesses he minds.

He enters dreams in unexpected guises
Suggesting jungles, jungle laughter, screams,
Telephone calls, pursuits and wild surprises,
Desperate croquet games and froggy streams.

A noise of idling river water comes
Across the cindered yard that's his demesne
And qualifies his busy to's and from's,
Mumbling of spongy pastures, far and green.

A solitary streetcar, deep in town,
Pesters the late sky with electric sparks.
Behind a million windows, Sleep, the clown,
Draws out his turn. The cats are in the parks.

AFTER THUNDER

In pools the city realigns itself
But wrong way to. There is a smell of earth,
A smell of thunder, still, in the ecstatic air
After the passion and flood of August rain.

These pleasures come by streetfuls, they
Come in excess, as though they did not care,
And overwhelm us; they bear an edge of pain
Which pierces us.

The city, now, washed by a summer shower,
Offers such overwhelming careless pleasure:
Pools on the pavement, creeks along the lane,
An air so sweet among the boughs and bricks
That only birds, who aren't afraid of gods
And have no language, give the time a voice
Which pierces us: the ecstatic edge of pain.

TIME IN A PUBLIC WARD

As life goes on to worse and worse
The bed beside me calls the nurse
And says, It's getting worse, I guess.
She makes the worse a little less
By needle. Soon along the wall
Another bed puts in a call.

After pills the lights go down;
The walls turn grey and pink and brown.
Time passes. All at once a jet
Of orange lights a cigarette
Within whose glow a caverned eye
Watches the cinder burn and die.

The walls go back to grey and pink
And brown again. One hears a sink
And low voices, rustling feet;
There's music somewhere, late and sweet.
Clocks in the town put by the night
Hour by hour, ticked and right.

KIND OFFICES

Andrew, an understanding boy,
Helps Cathleen; he gets her toy
Or puts her dolly in her hand;
He sits her up, he makes her stand;
He picks her dolly up again
And gives it back to her and then
Re-erects her on her feet.
In all he does his air is sweet,
Olympian, perhaps; his smile
Is heaven's blandest. She, meanwhile,
Is rage itself. I cannot tell
Her rage: she's brimstone pits and hell.

RAIN

Yellow lights in the dark
And streets weak with rain and men;
I'd rather never have been born
Than feel the way I do again.

I'd rather never see the light
Than see it through a window pane
On which I feel myself run down
In weakness, with the drops of rain.

WAR ON THE PERIPHERY

Around the battlements go by
Soldier men against the sky,
Violent lovers, husbands, sons,
Guarding my peaceful life with guns.

My pleasures, how discreet they are!
A little booze, a little car,
Two little children and a wife
Living a small suburban life.

My little children eat my heart;
At seven o'clock we kiss and part,
At seven o'clock we meet again;
They eat my heart and grow to men.

I watch their tenderness with fear
While on the battlements I hear
The violent, obedient ones
Guarding my family with guns.

REST HOUR

Noises coming down the stairs,
Thumping noises, bumping chairs,
Roaring, whistling, muscle testing
Tell the hour of Andrew's resting.

Giant in his moods and grace,
Giant blood and giant pace
He fills the hour after lunch
Fighting gods with heave and punch.

Grievous energies of growth,
Storms of pride and tides of sloth
Sweep across his giant soul
Against the gods, the small and whole,

In vain, heroically in vain;
Noises come downstairs again.
The gods lunge and leap away
Knowing they'll win, but not today.

CATHLEEN SWEEPING

The wind blows, and with a little broom
She sweeps against the cold clumsy sky.
She's three years old. What an enormous room
The world is that she sweeps, making fly
A little busy dust! And here am I
Watching her through the window in the gloom
Of this disconsolate spring morning, my
Thoughts as small and busy as her broom.

Do I believe in her? I cannot quite.
Beauty is more than my belief will bear.
I've had to borrow what I think is true:
Nothing stays put until I think it through.
Yet, watching her with her broom in the dark air,
I give it up. Why should I doubt delight?

MONEY IN POCKET

I've got money in my pockets,
Excellent pockets because there's money in them;
I cant feel low while there's paper for my fingers
In my excellent pockets, Caesar's mark on it.

I've got children in my rooms,
Blood-borne hostages, arrows from my side:
I cant sleep heavy while they're breathing in their beds
Who burst through my passageways and grow me back to earth.

I've got time in my clocks
And beer in my cellar and spiders in my windows:
I cant spend time nor drink all the beer
And I feel in the spread web the spider's small eye.

THE LIFE IN AUGUST

The prospect is of ribbed clouds across the sky
And blue water when the air is clear and the weather fine all day;
Then, when the rocks are hot, the turtles doze
And at night frogs pontificate across the bay in sonorous dignity.

Islands are bent then, when the wind is westerly,
And the sky stands in green-blue, blue-green
Over the everlasting swishing of the whitecaps.

CATS

I Pussy's caught a baby bird
    And she's so pleased with it
She's purring as she's never purred;
    She lets it go a bit
As though she held it by a thread
Or love, perhaps. Above her head

The air's extravagant with grief.
    The season over all
Is prodigal of bone and leaf
    And feathers too; the fall
Scatters the birds and leaves at last.
Eat it, pussy, life flies past!

II Every yard has a cat these days
    Watching, footing, blinking;
Every tree has a cheeky squirrel,
    Seemingly all unthinking,
    Going his squirrel ways
As though no cat in the world were waiting, slinking.

Life is exquisite when it's just
    Out of reach by a bound
Of filigree jaws and delicate paws
    That feel their points in the ground,
    That drop their drips in the dust ...
Pounce! Up the tree again! The tails whip round.

FLIGHT

All day long the clouds go by,
Early winter clouds, not high;
Wide as charity they range,
Restless, regimented, strange.

From my neighbourhood a crow
Takes it in his head to go
Somewhere else he knows about;
Melancholy bird, no doubt.

Up he rises from a tree
Where a yellow leaf or three
Still hang on for hanging's sake,
Tug their yellow stems and shake.

Caw! he cries, as though he knew
Something worth his while to do
In an empty tree elsewhere;
Flap! he takes his blackness there.

Me too! I should like to fly
Somewhere else beneath the sky,
Happy though my choice may be
Empty tree for empty tree.

THE CRUISING AUK

Questioning Mr. Murple
I found that he agreed
– We all, in fact, agreed –
It was a splendid auk
Flying across the sky.

And such a pleasure it is to see an auk
Shadow the sun with his little wings and his beak,
Going about his business in the air
Or hurrying home, or merely taking the weather!

Surely his eye belittles our despair,
Our unheroic mornings, afternoons
Disconsolate in the echo-laden air –
Echoes of trumpet noises, horses' hooves.

Splendid, however, we can
Rejoice in him, cruising there:
He is our uncle, and lo,
O Mr. Murple, O beloved friends,
Airborne!

IN THE POND

The pond in Mr. Murple's yard
    I feel it in my shoes;
Deep in my shoes I feel the pond
    In Mr. Murple's yard.

And how much wiser shall I be
    When I am in the pond?
When over me the sky is wet
    Shall I much wiser be?

A little bird beside the pond
    Angles his eye at me
Where very deep and very wet
    I lie, beneath the pond.

Well may the bird look down on me,
    Cocking his little eye;
He knows the way to Paradise
    But he does not know me.

A MYSTIC OF THE AIR AGE

As though to pass beyond herself
Mrs. McGonigle emplaned;
Behold her from her pantry shelf
Remote, poised in a speck, contained!

Speeding, speeding, ah behold
Mrs. McGonigle afar
In the intense inane and cold
Where disembodied spirits are!

Extreme is yonder stratosphere,
The uttermost and least of air,
And while our mortal clay is here
Mrs. McGonigle's is there.

ICE AT LAST

When ice at last has come across the pond
And the old angry sun dismissed himself
In roasted lobster colour;
When trees all bare divaricate their twigs
Against the salmon sky and then go black,
This is when the accomplished Mr. Murple
Splendid on skates comes forth to spin the night
Upon his arms outstretched and whirling eyeballs.

Coffee drinkers fill the hut with steam;
They warm themselves within against the cold
That creaks without and circumvents the light,
While Mr. Murple, in a cloud of frost
Centripetal,
Turns on his pivot skates the captive sky.

LIGHT LITERATURE

In the short sharp winter twilight
   When beans are in to cook
Edward under the trilight
   Reads a detective book.

He scares his inner workings
   Into a fluid state
And his outer same to jerkings
   And yet he sits up late

Reading of nervous habits
   And nervous ways to kill;
The suspects breed like rabbits
   Till all the rooms are still.

Then up he creeps to his attic
   Feeling his instincts near
As a radio feels its static
   And voices mixed and queer.

Life has ebbed to a flicker
   Of neon light in town;
The attic waits with a snicker
   To bed poor Edward down.

RAPTURE

Sweet lovers lie around the bay
Lapped in each other's arms:
Mrs. Beleek with Dr. Gay,
Joad with Miss Decharmes,
Snug in their cabins tucked away
Sleeping the early hours of day.

Fishes within the burnished bay
Dimple the face thereof
Leaping to enter, as they may,
The mirror world above;
Delicate fishes, how they play!
Rapture is in the air today.

FUN

Elaine sleeps in her maiden bed
Still as the moonlight overhead;
Dreaming, across the way from her
Mrs. McGonigle's boarders stir;
Innocent boarders' dreams are sweet
Of beauty sleeping across the street.

Only the innocent have fun:
The beautiful Elaine is one,
The boarders are another seven;
Never a thought they give to heaven
Until their innocence is through.
Ah then, sweet joy, sweet grief, adieu!

POOR EDWARD

Whose hat is moving on the water's face
Making towards the sea a doubtful pace?
Poor Edward's, I'm disconsolate to say,
He owed me twenty dollars, by the way.
I look along the darkening bank and wonder
How Edward and his wisdom came asunder.

The air grows cool, the crowd has partly gone;
The lights begin to fidget off and on;
The boats kechunk and creak as to and fro
And up and down and through the bridge they go
Fishing, fishing where the water's deep
For Edward and his trouble, sound asleep.

QUEENS AND DUCHESSES

Miss Belaney's pleasure is vast,
    Indeed it fills the night;
She doesn't remember who kissed her last
    But he did it good, all right.

She doesn't remember who broke her flowers
    When her fastenings came undone;
Her lipstick hasn't been straight for hours,
    She's had a night of fun.

Around her head is a haze of gold,
    Pleasure shines in her dress
Illuminating its every fold,
    Blessing each drunken tress.

Queens, queens, a little bit lighter
    They go, than we of the town;
And jewelled duchesses, grander and brighter
    When they step down, step down.

Queens, queens, they smile and go,
    Their loves and deaths are sad;
Duchesses now and again stoop low;
    Miss Belaney is bad.

HOME AGAIN

Home again at four o'clock and up the sleeping stair,
Darkness in my loving parts, serpents in my hair,
Having been a reigning moon for half the loving night
And then a piece of iced cake for any god to bite;
Now I am a bent doll, I shed my silky stuff
And soon I'll be a sleeping heart. The gods got enough.

ANNABELLE

Annabelle has yellow teeth
And solid rubber underneath,
Golden polish on her toes
And pink and purple underclothes.
Nothing effervesces quite
As Annabelle when she is tight.

ON THE PORCH

What's on your mind tonight,
    Mary bloody Jane?
Why do you click the light
    Laughing like a drain?
Gentlemen are a dying race,
    Click it on again!

It isn't the way you walk
    Drifting down the street,
It isn't the way you talk
    Doing things with your feet,
It isn't the way you friz your hair
    And make your odours sweet.

A fellow's not made of glass
    Nor he isn't made of steel,
Some of the time he's an ass
    Some of the time he's a heel
Some of the time he's a shot down god
    And that's the way I feel.

ELAINE IN A BIKINI

Mrs. McGonigle's boys enjoy the sun
By gogglesful, & stare along the beach
Whose innocence is almost all Elaine,
    Almost, but not quite, all.

Felicitously she comes in every eye
Bending her knees and tender finger nails
While the incalculable strings gather in
    What's hers to gather in.

Her feet entice themselves across the sands
Down to the water's edge, & the old sea
Fumbles about the naked afternoon
    As though in paradise.

I am felicitous too, on the bright shore
Waiting for darkness with the roving boys
And all but gathered in myself with strings,
    What's mine to gather in.

ELAINE IN A BIKINI

Mrs. McGonigle's boys enjoy the sun
By gogglesful, and stare along the beach
Whose innocence is almost all Elaine,
    Almost, but not quite, all.

Felicitously she comes in every eye
Bending her knees and tender finger nails
While the incalculable strings gather in
    What's hers to gather in.

Her feet entice themselves across the sands
Down to the water's edge, and the old sea
Fumbles about the naked afternoon
    As though in paradise.

I am felicitous too, on the bright shore
Waiting for darkness with the roving boys
And all but gathered in myself with strings,
    What's mine to gather in.

THE ROLL CALL

Names of my aunts in order: Mrs. Balls,
Mrs. McGonigle, Lou, old Great-aunt Hairy,
Gentle, unmentionable Aunt Beleek
Who's intricate in underwear and shoes,
Who's fickle in them, fiddled, fled, forgotten –
My sweetest aunt, Beleek, and slightly rotten.

The roll call comforts me. Bless Aunt McGonigle,
Bless Mrs. Balls,
Bless all my aunts! I name their splendid names,
My queens of air, my dolls,
And my mortality, alas!

Day light passes. Night light passes too,
And all my aunts, however full in sight,
However giant-bowelled, -breasted, -sinewed,
Will founder, as the suns behind the chimneys;
Nor even fickle Aunt Beleek will linger,
Singled out by the somewhat smelly finger
Of recollection, poking among the drawers.
How can my wormy shelves and cupboards keep her
That have so many wormy things to keep?

MUSIC ON THE WATER

Saturday night she comes in her little boat
When the air is warm on the smoky river, afloat,
Making her presence felt in her flickering oars:
A journeying wound between the fragile shores.

Nights of splendour she's been to splendid men,
Swallowed them whole and spit them up again,
After which they've forgotten her perhaps –
As though she might have remembered them, poor chaps.

Now they're distributed about the town,
Two in a meeting, one in a dressing gown,
One in a hospital bed with stinking bones,
One in a radio drama, making groans.

One is a kind, white-eyebrowed public man,
Used to write poems and at times still can;
Fame is his breakfast food and evening prayer;
Saturday night he dozes in his chair.

Out on the skin of water she sings a song,
Sweet but a little bit flat and sometimes wrong;
Under the bridge it wobbles as she goes by
And wastes away in the willow trees and the sky.

The song she sings is a Pentecostal hymn
According to which Earth's glories are rather dim
Whereas the rewards of the just are very bright;
Low kind of song, but it serves her turn all right.

ART AND LIFE

Sadie McGonigle, Mrs. McGonigle's daughter,
Is in a state of art from head to foot;
She's spent the afternoon with suds and water
And creams and mud; her lines and points are put
And every inch is tender to the view –
Elegant work of art and artist too.

Sweet love, that takes a master piece like this
And rumples it and tumbles it about,
Why can he not be happy with a kiss?
He turns the shimmering object inside out
And all for life, that's enemy to art.
Now where's your treasure, little scented heart?

THE QUEEN OF LOP

She works all day at a big machine that lops and lops and lops;
At five o'clock she does her face and the big machine it stops;
Home again on a public bus she goes to her little flat,
Cooks a chop and forgets the lop and the wash-up and all that.

The days go on as they always do and the evenings pass in fun;
Edward comes with his gloomy face, he makes the hours run;
Maybe they watch a picture show in the lovely dark abyss
And if Edward's good and the show is good it's the next best thing to bliss.

The wind that overcasts the lake and wears across the hills
Rattles itself among the city's roofs and window sills;
Around her bed the noises come, they give her dreams a steer:
The little flat becomes a boat on the ocean dark and queer.

The big machine is aboard the boat and so is Edward's face;
The shores go back, the thunders come, Leviathan gives chase;
On and on through the dreadful hours the winds and waters run
Until the walls wake up again and the curtains catch the sun.

The waters ebb from the papered room, the air is filled with light;
Bacon smells and coffee smells begin the day's delight;
On to the public bus again and on to the big machine
Whose lop is a well-run kingdom, ruled by a decorous queen.

A SAINT

Around the corner, down the street,
I overtook and turned to greet,
Taking his troubles for a walk
My old friend Boom. We had a talk
And as it happened we agreed
On many things, but on the need
Especially of mental strife
And of a whole new source of life.
The evening shone like polished brass.
Alas, said mournful Boom, alas!
While all around the chickadees
Hunted for bugs among the trees.

Boom is a saint, his sufferings
Put him in the know of things,
Teach him what is what and what
In spiritual things is not.
And when he looks upon us all
His heart contracts into a ball
Which is the perfect form of grief;
Its perfectness provides relief.

Another kind of perfect form
Provides relief for Uncle Norm
But Uncle Norm is not a saint
And neither I suppose I aint.

DUST

Old Mrs. McWhirter is musty dusty old;
Down she goes to her cellar, it's full of bugs and cold;
Up she goes to her bottles, they're pink and green and brown;
Everywhere is a hairpin, they're always coming down.

Out from her dusty nightgown her dusty angels creep;
They harp and sing in the twilight before she goes to sleep
Sweet notes on the staircase that tinkle high and fall
Among the dusty shadows from the cellarway and hall.

Nobody knows but the angels how deep the dark goes down;
They wont tell Mrs. McWhirter, they flash their wings and clown;
Mrs. McWhirter mutters, the angels tease and scold;
A glory comes from their feathers, their voices ring like gold.

Dear Mrs. McWhirter, I wish she wouldn't die
In the dusty way she's planned it: I wish the Lady Sky,
Having come home from her orbits and interstellar space,
Would set aside in Eternity a homey dusty place

Where Mrs. might spat with her angels as thoughts together spat
In the dome of Eternal Wisdom, under the Eternal Hat;
But the bugs and bottles and hairpins will have to stay behind
Because Eternity's stuffy, and perhaps a bit unkind.

ROSES

Among the roses down behind the house
Snip snap snip! go the little cutting pliers;
Sweet Miss Knit, who is a kind of a mouse,
Is gathering buds and blooms for Mr. Byers.
Mr. Byers is a kind of a hungry cat
Whose hunger somehow is not for sweet Miss Knit;
She loves his magnificent person, which is fat,
And longs to be devoured, every bit.

Ah roses, roses on Mr. Byers' table,
That lean your thorns above the polished wood!
Miss Knit would borrow your deaths if she were able
To darken her small heart, discreet and good.
And yet the room's mahogany-deep light
And all the little rainbows in the glass
Seem to surround her movements with delight
And watch her mouse's footsteps as they pass.

NOCTAMBULE

Mr. Murple's got a dog that's long
And underslung and sort of pointed wrong;
When daylight fades and evening lights come out
He takes him round the neighbour lawns about
To ease himself and leak against the trees,
The which he does in drops and by degrees
Leaving his hoarded fluid only where
Three-legged ceremonious hairy care
Has been before and made a solemn sign.
Mythology, inscrutable, canine,
Makes his noctambulation eloquent
And gives a power of meaning to his scent
That all who come and sniff and add thereto
And scratch the turf, may know they have to do
With Mr. Murple's underslung long dog,
His mark, his manifesto and his log.

THE BULGE

Nobody knows what's growing in Bridget,
   Nobody knows whose is, what's more:
Maybe a beauty queen, maybe a midget,
   Maybe a braided bloke to stand by the door.

Lovely full Bridget, her eyes are like figs,
   Her belly's an ocean, heaving with fish,
Her heart is a barnyard with chickens and pigs,
   Her outside's a banquet, her tongue is a dish.

Something enormous is bulging in Bridget –
   A milkman, a postman, a sugar-stick, a slop,
An old maid, a bad maid, a doughhead, a fidget,
   Multiple sweet Bridget, what will she drop?

A HAPPY GHOST

As though he'd overslept he died
And when he did he filled the room
With the dampness of his pride
Like the smell of bloom in hothouses

Wherein are growing many droopy plants:
A palm tree, a banana tree and ferns,
Orchids and other petal skins, and toads.

Meanwhile his little ghost infects the roads,
A happy ghost, whom everything enchants,
Bedded not yet among the bones and urns.

DOMESTIC

A man should build himself a house and put himself inside
And fill it full of furniture, and get himself a bride
To fill it full of cooking smells and pickle smells and wit
And all in pleasure breed it full, and make a nest of it.

It wont work, I've asked around, although it sounds so nice
  Miss
Belaney and Miss Decharmes and Dorothy say no dice.

ESCAPE

Fleeing from Mrs. McGonigle, Mr. Smith
Took refuge in a public telephone booth
Whence he rang, as he always did, forthwith,
The gospel tabernacle, home of Truth.

Mrs. McGonigle meanwhile searched the streets
Asking herself as she did so why she did.
His life with her she knew was a nest of sweets
From which he beat it, now and again, and hid.

And every time he ended up on his knees
Among his burning friends at Gospel Hall
Who put his soul through fire and gave it ease
With balm from the Apostles, especially Paul.

These were his most exciting days, no doubt,
Groaning and urging a consciousness of sin,
But Mrs. McGonigle always found him out
Sooner or later, and motherly gathered him in.

Truly a man is never lonely here
And least of all at the moment of wild escape
In the telephone booth, a moment of bliss and fear
Between this world and the next, between fire and rape.

MRS. McGONIGLE ON DECORUM

Dont be nervous, Mary Anne,
    Dont be nervous, dear!
Carry a little water can
    To catch the quiet tear.

Dont let anyone see it there,
    Dont let anyone know;
Put it away in your clothes somewhere,
    Dump it before you go.

Do as the lovely ladies do,
    Mark the words of the gents,
Dont run off when you're spoken to,
    Dont start arguments!

Ah, that my hours beside the sink
    Were printed in a book!
Many who tremble on the brink
    Would take a second look.

Dont be nervous, Mary Anne,
    Everyone else, you know,
Carries a little water can
    And doesn't let it show.

LIFE FROM A GOLDFISH BOWL

Mr. Murple called upon his mother
Bringing a bottle of gin for Mother's Day;
They tolerate, indeed they love each other
And often rub each other the right way.
'Mother,' he said, 'I brought you this here gin,
Product of Messrs. Moult, Moultville, you know.
Look at the fancy piece of glass it's in!
Times have been extra good to Moult and Co.'

'Drat the flies, they're awful bad this year!'
She said, waving a big one from her nose.
'What have you got there? Bless your heart, my dear!
Put it on the piano, by the rose.
A nice red rose to show I'm still alive:
Fifty cents they asked me for it, thieves!
Yellow to show you're dead is fifty-five
All done up in ferny things and leaves.'

What a life for a goldfish, day and night
Who fins in Mr. Murple's mother's bowl!
He gets a bit of flat stuff for a bite
Maybe, or maybe ant eggs – eaten whole –
And notes the goings-on with goggle face
Of all the world around about in air:
Of Mr. Murple with his gloves and grace
Coming with gifts for mother in her lair.

FLOWERS AND CHILDREN

Mrs. Beleek, an aunt of ours,
Lifts her behind among her flowers
Putting ingenious stuff around
To baffle bugs and coax the ground.

What does she think about all day?
Children, that's what, that come her way:
Bobby, Ronald, Elizabeth-Anne,
Pie-faced Linda and sweet Diane.

Little Diane, to cite a case:
What a pleasure to, well, erase!
And Linda, how bumpable-off, with skill,
Over the bathroom window sill.

From any corner around the lot
Neatly a hopeful might be shot,
Neatly to bite the bordered dust
Treated for fungus rot and crust.

Heaven visits on Aunt Beleek
Every once or twice a week
Moments almost too bright to bear.
Bless her old heart, she should take care!

THE HERO'S KITCHEN

A seal of holiness descends
   Upon the kitchen floor;
Mrs. Belaney and her friends
   Knit and discuss the war.
Mrs. Belaney has a son
   – Had, I should say, perhaps –
Who deeds of gallantry has done,
   Him and some other chaps.

Into his hand the Seraphim
   Gave the destructive sword,
Beckoning as they did in him
   Creation's restless lord.
Fire and blood became his trade;
   Gentle and clumsy one
At home he was, but on parade
   Creation's restless son.

Mrs. Belaney feels the wall
   Rustle with angel wings;
Tears of a sacred nature fall
   Into the knitting things.
Then begins tea, and cakes and pies
   Muffle the ladies' chat;
Out of the shadows angel eyes
   Bless the dear comfort of that.

THE DUFUFLU BIRD

The call of the dufuflu bird
  For which I have an ear
Falls like the uncreating word,
  But only some can hear.

And often at the droop of day
  When evening grumbles in
The great dufuflu seems to bray
  Above the traffic's din.

We, maybe, when we're on a walk
  And maybe feeling low
Hear an apocalyptic squawk
  And think it's time to go.

Our hearts respond, our souls respond,
  The very we of us
Takes off, as one might say, beyond,
  But then comes back, alas!

We hardly fuss, perhaps we pray
  – The timid drop a tear –
And go our uncomplaining way
  Keeping a wakeful ear

Hoping the great dufuflu bird
  May open up, and then
In such a voice as will be heard
  By us and all good men.

MR. GOOM

Earth fills her lap for Mr. Goom
With gifts, of which in studied measure
And with the *savoir-faire* of doom
He makes selection for his pleasure.

Yet life is often very sad
For Mr. Goom, he doesn't know
Whether it's really good or bad
Its sweetest moments sour so.

And though he cherishes his gifts
– His lovely clothes, his lovely friends –
His dilettante attention shifts
From time to time to mortal ends

And then he finds he needs a drink
Or else a Turkish bath to chase
His apperception from the brink
Of darkness to a brighter place.

Always around the door he knows
The brink of darkness drops away
And sure enough the door will close
After him over it one day.

The tears I shed for Mr. Goom
Are soft in character and fine
As his own amiable perfume:
They fall between his fate and mine.

PASTORALE

The grasshopper does not so free
The silly summer time dispense
As Mr. Murple in a tree
Playing upon wind instruments.

He fills the air with ornaments
Trilling and running gracefully,
Oblivious of audience
And in his improvising free.

The snake, the frog, the bumblebee
And other forest residents
Hark to his music solemnly,
Soothed to a charming diffidence.

IN IT

The world is a boat and I'm in it
Going like hell with the breeze;
Important people are in it as well
Going with me and the breeze like hell –
It's a kind of a race and we'll win it.
Out of our way, gods, please!

The world is a game and I'm in it
For the little I have, no less;
Important people are in it for more,
They watch the wheel, I watch the door.
Who was the first to begin it?
Nobody knows, but we guess.

The world is a pond and I'm in it,
In it up to my neck;
Important people are in it too,
It's deeper than this, if we only knew;
Under we go, any minute –
A swirl, some bubbles, a fleck....

WET

It's rained sort of day after day
Till the bottom is, as it were, wet;
My feelings are all washed away
But something is left of me yet

And whatever the something may be
I take it to eat and to bed
Because after all it's still me –
Come rain, wash the lot! Let's be dead.

EATING FISH

Here is how I eat a fish
  – Boiled, baked or fried –
Separate him in the dish,
    Put his bones aside.

Lemon juice and chive enough
    Just to give him grace,
Make of his peculiar stuff
    My peculiar race.

Through the Travellers' Hotel
    From the sizzling pan
Comes the ancient fishy smell
    Permeating man.

May he be a cannier chap
    Altered into me,
Eye the squirming hook, and trap,
    Choose the squirming sea.

O EARTH, TURN!

The little blessed Earth that turns
Does so on its own concerns
As though it weren't my home at all;
It turns me winter, summer, fall
Without a thought of me.

I love the slightly flattened sphere,
Its restless, wrinkled crust's my here,
Its slightly wobbling spin's my now
But not my why and not my how:
My why and how are me.

O EARTH, TURN!

The little blessed Earth that turns
Does so on its own concerns
As though it weren't my home at all;
It turns me winter, summer, fall
Without a thought of me.

I love the slightly flattened sphere,
Its restless, wrinkled crust's my here,
Its slightly wobbling spin's my now
But not my why and not my how:
My why and how are me.

MAIL-ORDER CATALOGUE

A paper land where death dont seem to come,
Where flannelette pyjamas, wreathed in smiles,
And ladies' corsets, smug as chewing gum,
Dwell overleaf from remedies for piles;

Where medicines to keep the stork at bay
– Flushed in the gents' long woollen underwear –
Offer themselves as well to passion's prey
As to the fruitful housewife, taking care.

Music of hi- and medium-fi degree,
Sump pumps, rubber gloves, and tires,
Castrators, bottle-warmers, lingerie,
Everything heart demands, or hand requires.

In spring and fall, when serious young men
Comfort themselves that all that lives must die,
Tax and the teeming catalogue again
Come round, and give mortality the lie.

Home Free

UNDER THE TREE

1 Hanging makes us one,
    I a hangman, you a hanging judge
    Meet under the hanging tree
    For the hard work that is waiting to be done
    And the hanging tree broods over you and me.

    I rise up in the morning and make my bed,
    Feed myself and discipline myself
    In the discipline by which my children are fed,
    I keep unwelcome thoughts out of my head,
       Get on with the day's work
    Thanking God for the backwater I am in,
       My even disposition
       That holds life at arm's length,
       Sense of humour,
       Conscience that lets me sleep at night
       And eat by day,
    And if sometimes I get an awful fright
    That takes my hunger away
    I can pray and pray,
       Make promises,
    And all in all I seem to be here to stay.

    You would not recognize me as the hangman
    Nor yourself as the hanging judge
    Nor either of us as the judge's dear old mistress
       Or the condemned man's dimwitted mother
       Or the butcher who butchers for the last meal;
    We hardly know each other
    But here we meet, under the hanging tree
    And a hard work is waiting to be done.

2 The tree is beautiful
That felled and hewn out along the grain
Becomes the structure, lofty, beautiful,
On which the condemned man is lifted up.

And the lime stones that build the prison wall
Cut and quarried out along the grain
    Are grey and beautiful,
Grey stones with the grain of ancient trees,
    Veins of ancient leaves
Chambers of architectural oozy creatures
    Embedded in their stuff.
They rest along the earth in stony levels,
Barred by windows, roofed by a stony roof,
Their fabric rising grey in the changing sky
    Hardly changing with its changes
    Keeping its stone mood
And roofing in the lifted hanging tree.

The judge is a limestone judge
    With chambered ancient levels in his mind,
    Veiny and fossil creatures in his soul;
In the Great War he was a gallant soldier,
Destroyed single-handed an enemy pill-box
With a Mills bomb, pushing it over the sill;
    Rescued an enemy nco under fire,
    Was decorated twice before he was twenty.
That was his war. Peace has brought him down
To money in traction, money in natural gas,
Big marriage. Death of a coward son
Heaved him and tore him like a birth.

He is kind as we would want to be kind
   Knows more than we know,
And he has consented to be our judge
    After a stern life as befits our justice,
    A sentimental life as befits our justice,
A steady voice of a life whose tones speak
The steady words of our law to the hanging tree.

3 Children's eyes uncover a new thing
   Wherever they look; the world unlocks
And opens hugely as they peer into it;
Yet every far horizon is no farther
Than the fetch of their eyes.

It is a giant world, magic and real,
With candelabra and branchy hanging trees
And dark holes that lead away to the black;
A hungry world, heart-eater of a world,
And yet a gorgeous-handed, a glad giver,
Extravagant over-giver of all imaginable things.

Children's roads lead all the way out to the edge
Through tall woods and wastes of metal and glass.
Electric eyes watch them, ogres are on their marches,
Yet this is true so long as childhood lasts
That every watched road has a secret way out.

4 At the high altar and other less orthodox places
  Amid incense, candle-smoke, odours of heavenly bliss
    And other less orthodox odours,
  Prayers are said for this hanging;
    And there is serious talk
    In little groups
  And many think it has been good
  Because God knows hanging is a prayerful thing.

  Others think of other prayerful things:
    Staggering needs of the world,
    Explosions, statistics,
    Bad news about the flock,
  And the murder was mean and casual,
  A young punk and an aged cigar-store keeper,
  He robbed the old lady and beat her and stabbed her with scissors
    And she lived for two days;
  Is it Godly to pray about such a thing?

5 The faithful bells join with the noises of town
   And the electronic chimes make a joyful noise;
   The condemned man's aunt comes from church and settles down
   To an afternoon in the living room with the boys.

   Capital punishment is a thing of the past
   They all agree, left over from barbarous days,
   And it ought to be abolished and abolished fast
   Before poor whosit comes to his time and pays.

   But it's already far too late says whosit's aunt,
   And it's never anything else but far too late;
   You think you want to do something, but you cant,
   And after you've smelled the rope you believe in fate.

   The boys all bleed around her, the longlegged boys,
   Sneering at fate. Who believes in fate? they sneer.
   But fate believes in the boys and their sneering noise,
   Their longlegged ploys and their notions soaked in beer.

6 The rope waits in air,
   Chaplain waits, prison officials wait,
   Newsmen with weary eyes
   Wait, hunching their collars up
       As winter birds hunch on chimney tops;
   And the apparatus of cleanliness waits
       And the keepers by the door,
   And the doctor who knows when a body dies:
   Stink of cleanliness makes their nostrils sore.

   For there is always something to wait for.
       Prisoners wait
       Watching their bars
       As they always wait,
   Knowing
   Watching
   Listening:
       The clock bears down on the waiting.

   How does it get done when it does get done?
       Somehow the wait must come to the event:
   Does the clock bring it on?

   There is a man to bring it on
   And for the moment he is you and me,
   Here we meet, under the hanging tree,
       And we wait
       And he waits
   And the clock bears down on our waiting.

7 God's good kind Earth, God's manybosomed Earth,
 God's suffering ugly cunning beautiful
   Wounded creature of Earth,
 The pit whence we were dug,
 The garden in which we grope
   For love;
 Kind Earth, our gorgeousness of blood,
 Our fleeting pain of birdsong,
 Our poised in air, our footsore, delicate,
 Our lifted up in grief, our loosed in death,
   Carrion;
 Darktongued Earth, tell our deeds to the dark.

FIELDS

Wild apple trees grow round the fields,
   Hay fields and oat fields,
   And fallow fields, pasture fields,
And small rain-dark elm trees
Cling to the edges of the fields.

Underneath the clinging trees
Dark shadows form themselves
   Lingering with the sun's delay,
   Dark as earth, dark as death,
Around the summer-bulging fields.

HONEY

In summer when the fields are sweet
With clover flowers and buckwheat
And vetch, and when the slopes are rich
With goldenrod, and every ditch
Is thick with prickly, fuzzy bloom,
Out through the season's long perfume
By ones and broken companies
Go Farmer Elliott's honey bees.

And if you listen in the heat
You will hear their brittle wings beat
Not very far above the ground
With an unceasing summer sound
As forth they go to plants and vines
And back again in busy lines
Giving their undistracted lives
To cramming Farmer Elliott's hives.

A worker's work is four weeks long
Or five or six if one is strong
Of flying out and back again,
So go its bee three-score and ten;
Its glassy wings bring honey home
And pollen for the honeycomb
Until they tatter, and it lies
A honey-cumbered heap and dies.

Earth gathers in again her sweet
And wax from its decaying feet
And takes her poison from its sting,
Its secret, sweetest offering
And her most intimate of powers,
The distillation of her flowers
Which it in death gives back to her
With its dead bones and wings and fur.

Between the hives the honeyed air
Drifts with the sweetness of despair,
And homing bees bombard their town
Like spent gold bullets dropping down:
Thick they go out and thick they come,
Around their narrow doors they hum
And all the business within
Hums with a thousand-bodied din.

When Farmer Elliott goes among
His bees he is not often stung,
They work with single-minded care
And never look to see him there;
His pace is too benign and slow
For their sweet-centred minds to know,
And yet one melancholy bee
One day may dream of such as he.

LOPEY

We have a gentle neuter cat
Whose name is Lopey. He's a fat
Good-natured tabby, somewhat yellow;
In his own way, a handsome fellow;
Forthcoming whiskers, fearful eyes,
Tail that drops and goes angle-wise.
He watches corners in the house
As though to concentrate on mouse
But his grey matter is not good,
It's full of holes, like wormy wood,
In which his notions go astray
Or, as it were, just leak away.

Lopey rests with one cocked ear
Because the Enemy is near
And vigilant to do him hurt;
And so his peace is all alert.
But then, because he is not wise,
He's always taken by surprise;
When his perch seems most secure,
Approaches watched and rearguard sure,
Eyelids burdened by the weight
Of creature confidence in fate,
The heavens give, and with a whack
The Enemy is on his back.
Howls of fear and snarls of grief,
The Worst is on him, like a thief,
Worse than his nightmares, flesh-hooks bared.
It finds his bosom unprepared.

His mother cat's a tortoise shell
Who's fought the world and knows it well,
Not all whose cleanliness of fur
And slenderness of bones, nor her
Disdainful gentleness of pace
Nor pussy-catness of her face
Temper the matriarchal laws
Sheathed in her feline lips and paws.
Her son's uncomplaining stare
Is sometimes more than she can bear
And then the laws' uncovered points
Strike terror into Lopey's joints;
They savage in him, tooth and nail,
The world's uncomprehending male.

But other times, perhaps a night
In winter when outdoors is white,
After her day beside the heat,
A ragbag cat, inert, effete,
His mother wakes to have some fun
And play tag with her big dumb son;
Round the table, round the chairs,
Up the curtains, up the stairs,
Hitting, hissing, leaping, crashing,
Resting, ears flat back, tails lashing,
Cleaning paws and searching fleas,
At ease, as gods may be at ease
Before they strike. The whirl begins
Like sparks again. Electric skins.

Peace is in excess, indoors
On days not frightened by the roars,
Not made disastrous by the sweep
And clank of vacuum-cleaner; sleep
Then visits Lopey as he squats
At ease among the flower pots,
Whose earth and odour drowse the room.
Under the burden of this bloom
Lopey's big eyes grow small and droop.
His mother, on the bare back stoop
Shuts her own sphinx eyes up tight
Against the soul-corroding sight
Of her dumb offspring, warm, inside.
Cold and her cat contempt and pride
Delineate in every line
Her mood, in the cat-cold white sunshine.

VETERANS

There are seventy times seven kinds of loving
   None quite right:
One is of making, one of arguing,
   One of wheedling in the night
And all the others one can think of, none quite right.

They are all good,
   Paying attention, giving the low-down kiss;
Answering back in the heart is always good
   And coming out of a sulk is almost bliss.

There is a kind of loving in grass and weeds,
   One in brass beds, another in corridors;
An uncanny kind that turns away & bleeds
   And a gorgeous kind, practised by saints & bores.

They are all hard,
   All seventy times seven, hard as can be:
Veterans of loving are wary-eyed & scarred
   And they see into everything they see.

VETERANS

There are seventy times seven kinds of loving
    None quite right:
One is of making, one of arguing,
    One of wheedling in the night
And all the others one can think of, none quite right.

They are all good,
    Paying attention, giving the low-down kiss;
Answering back in the heart is always good
    And coming out of a sulk is almost bliss.

There is a kind of loving in grass and weeds,
    One in brass beds, another in corridors;
An uncanny kind that turns away and bleeds
    And a gorgeous kind, practised by saints and bores.

They are all hard,
    All seventy times seven, hard as can be:
Veterans of loving are wary-eyed and scarred
    And they see into everything they see.

Home Free

1 Morning

At half-past six a.m. the sun
Shines on the water tub
Outside the kitchen door,
And from the chicken run
Utters the matutinal squawk and roar
Of Mr. Murple's Red Rhode Island rooster,
Who walks among his hens as a storm of rain,
Shedding his bounty in a long-legged way,
And crested with the sun.
Listen! Across the fields of hay and grain
Mrs. McGonigle's Leghorn answers him,
His voice made melancholy by the dew.

Stentor to stentor call the warm day in
When things get done,
When webs dry up and flies get caught therein,
When ducks and pigs grow fat,
When, from behind the barn, the slobbering churn
Turns the sweet Brigid's morning into butter
And buttermilk;
When the sea smiles upon himself
And brings his fish-and-lobster water up,
And sea-weed water, up among the rocks
And having done so brings it back again;
When Mr. Murple reaches from the shelf
His adding machine, to add his business up.

How shall we count our blessings? Mr. Murple
May pick all day at his pocket adding machine,
Hearing the sea go splash among the rocks,
Nor leave out Brigid, by the chicken run
Whistling in the sunshine, nor forget
The ducks and pigs, nor the innumerable spiders
– Also a blessing, in a long-legged way –
And still not make the total right, not quite.

2 Evening

The sun goes down, the hens go up to roost;
The grass is quiet, but not so the hens.
Mr. Murple's adding machine is at rest,
And the sea's face is at rest, although his depths
Rankle with bulging eyes;
But here, above, affairs have all gone west
From off the surfaces of sea and land
Except from off the hens: Ladies! Girls!
Wherefore this cluck and feather?
Wherefore this social failure in the twilight?
The bugs are courting with their lights and cries
And eating one another, as they do
Earnestly, and with skill, and without recess.
Brigid is courting in her courting dress
And the hour is so beautiful and deep
That Mr. Murple is made morbid by it.
His heart goes splash among its utmost rocks
And so draws back, and then goes splash again
Uncomforted.

Home Free

The hour grows deeper still
And more beautiful. The stars glare out.
Whoever came up late among the hens
Has found her place at last and gone to sleep.
Brigid leans against the wall and smokes
And laughs, and her cigarette glares out,
And overhead the winking weather aircraft
Wings to the west, with his many instruments.
He seems alone up there, but he is warm.

Home Free

THE BARGAIN SALE

The time has come. I'm going to sell
My photograph of the abyss,
Which I've had framed to look like hell,
An *objet d'art* I wont much miss;
I have some other things as well
More or less obsolete like this,
Some have been treasures, some have not,
I'm putting prices on the lot.

Here is a thing a sage might wear
For queasy stomach, clammy palm,
Other forebodings of despair;
This is my mask of Stoic calm;
Aging, but still in good repair,
It's covered me from qualm to qualm,
But I've grown big or it's grown small,
Now it wont fit my case at all.

Among my handkerchiefs and scent
While I was rummaging one day
Look what I found: the sentiment
Embrace your Fate, like new, slight fray;
Here is an antique ornament
Some *weltanschauung* might well display;
Favourite item once upon
A time. Ah well, the sale is on.

Home Free

Why do I want to sell my stuff
In these exciting days? I know
That life is earnest, time is tough,
But me, I'm not, I'm soft and slow.
Look, I'm not asking half enough,
My prices are absurdly low,
Bargains out of this world are they;
Buy them, before they fade away.

Home Free

SLOE WHISKY

Distillers of sloe whisky
    around here
go about their back basement mystery
    year after year
and in the fall
when the price of sloes comes down
they syndicate and buy in quantity.

Then what do they do?
    God knows
how they hive in their back basements and tramp and brew
    and age the sloes
until the sweetness of their bitterness comes through.

So dire a sweetness
    finds its way
to the deliciousness of our incompleteness
and then it hurts
and lays our souls wide open.
    Never again! we say,
crying repentant tears
and comforted by the dignity of our weakness.

THE CREATURE'S CLAIM

I stare back at a gibbous moon and brood,
Hardly knowing the words that name my mood
Or the moon's mood, that shares the Earth with me,
Her stony stuff and creaturely history.

I brood over the creatureliness of Earth
This gibbous night, fifty years from my birth,
And feel her claim, not on my yielded life
But on my heart, cut out with a stone knife.

Home Free

OLD-FASHIONED CHORDS

The rain rains in its never-ending way
And someone is playing jazz in an empty hall
   Among the trees;
Mid-afternoon of a long day
And through the leaves come the old-fashioned chords.

The music comforts itself
For some old-fashioned nagging foolishness,
Confessing what no confessor will hear one say
   Not about sin or guilt
   Existence or any of that,
Just some remembering of good times gone
That wont come back again ever, gone to stay.

Home Free

PIED A TERRE

I sleep in a let bed
In a let room, down a corridor,
And thousands others like me overhead
And all around, sleep out their separate dooms
And breed separate dooms in all these rooms
Seduced by wall to wall carpet and perfumes.

I have had company too.
    The sweetness, the fastidiousness!
She came and went as hunger came and went.
And a blue neon light outside the window
    Came and went,
And all the sweet fastidiousness got spent.

I have another address
That only I know about, in the country,
An island with a cave, burnt-out fires and bones;
    No-one can get at me there, it is my own.
    No-one lets it me, I own it.
And I can be cruel as nature there, and alone.

Home Free

BICULTURAL

Ottawattawattawa
Mother of our country's law,
How your spiky womb does teem
Words that are not what they seem,
Words that stretch and words that shrink,
Words that hover on the brink,
Words that round the world resound
With a House of Commons sound
Noncommittal and profound.

Outtaouttaouttaoua
C'est un nom sauvage n'est-ce pas?
Oui, c'est ça, dat's has you say,
Moitiémoitié ben Français,
Alf an alf maudsits Anglais.

Ottawa
L'enfant éternel joue
Dans les rues tristes de ton Lower Town
Fifrant son fifre, mais nous ne dansons pas.
Les neiges descendent partout
Parmi tes toits, et font réjouir le soleil.
Never are your streets so gay
As when your brats come out in the cold to play
In the exquisite wind that hunts all day
And all night too, and searches out
The shivers in our hearts. It brings the terror
That whirls about Confederation Square
And blazes in the January sun.
Along comes spring and breaks up everything.
Out come the dynamiters on the ice
To let the waters loose
Which by and by fill up the sweet canal.

This is how love infiltrates Ottawa
Along the streets and out into the suburbs,
Up in the Chateau, down by the river mud,
Under the copper roofs where civil servants
Earn their most sacred pay
Love goes to work, like worms,
In the marrow of Ottawa's bones.

Ottawa
N'as-tu pas tes grandes saisons,
Tes longues soirées d'été?
Puis tes orages, tonnères, terminent tes paresses.
The lamps tremble all night long in your waters
After the rain, for the pullulation of your daughters.
Sometimes I float among your waterways
Feeling so insignificant and fine
That all my attitudes just fall away.
The murmur of decision, drifting down
From Parliament Hill, and from the cocktail lounges
Hardly entices me to take a stand.
I know that every corner of the country
Represents itself here most solemnly
To have its business done and make its voice
Audible in the councils of the world.
The ship of state is navigated here;
Canada is afloat as I am afloat
On her capital city's waters,
And where is she going? She is going round and round
Like the United States, but farther north.

Home Free

REMEMBRANCE

Every November eleventh after the leaves have gone,
After the heat of summer when the heats of winter come on,
Ghosts from all over the country drift to the capital then
To see what we do to remember, we left-over Ottawa men,
We veterans and near veterans left over from obsolete wars,
Hitler's war and the Kaiser's and that ancient one with the Boers;
They haunt Confederation Square to see what we do
But it cant be very exciting, there's never anything new;
Year after year we gather and shout commands in the Square,
Wait for the Governor General, say a few words of prayer,
Lay our wreaths in order, mothers and big shots first,
In memory of those who have made it to the other side of the worst
And left us righteous survivors in the world they thought they might save,
Blowing our bugles and noses and making ourselves feel brave,
And not only brave but prudent, and not only prudent but wise,
Go to sleep ghosts, we say, and wave our wise goodbyes.

THE ROYAL COMMISSION

They have named a royal commission
  To ask itself what for,
Which is a really deadly serious question,
  Never been asked before.

What does the commission do?
  Sits on its bottom and thinks,
Takes hearings, and worries its papers through
  And feeds itself and drinks.

Plenty to drink and to eat
  Is how the country is run;
Hungry and sober is merely confusion and defeat
  Besides not being much fun.

But what for?   what for?   what for?
  The commission has soaked its wits
And fed itself daily from nine to four,
  But none of its answers fits.

Never mind, the Queen's printer will gather
  It into a heavy book,
Purple prose, profundities and blather,
  Giving it a solemn look.

Who knows whether the question
  Is really asked or not?
The best brains in the country on the commission
  Are giving it a thought.

Here is a marvellous thing
  About the doings of men:
They all have to be done over from the beginning
  Over and over again.

SPRING MOON

Moon in a town sky,
Half shut, dark one way from the middle,
Above a creek with spring peepers.

Homeward all alone, after joy,
Hands in pockets, making a thoughtful way
Over the bridge, down the street.

No voices, no women,
Only peepers,
And a solemn unsteadiness of all things.

THE LILY POND

Down at the bottom of Third Avenue
Ottawa has a lily-pond on view,
Neat little stone-edged pond, just big enough
That a small wind will make its waters rough.
Down to it all the children come and play
So gleefully they seem to shut away
The old vehicular world that hurries by.
A willow tree leans out across the sky
And drops its hairy image in the pond,
And on the benches round it and beyond
Old men sit, and pregnant mothers sit
Taking their time, making the most of it.

Home Free

THE SIBERIAN OLIVE TREE

Walking upwind under Bronson Bridge
In winter time, thinking wintry thoughts,
I look through at a Siberian olive tree
That has been planted alongside the canal.

Trees are women, they bear God's earthy weight
In their branches.
They are rooted and wounded;
They lift their matrices in wounded air
And wound the earth with stone-destroying roots.

This is not an old woman olive tree
But a feathery lady;
Her black trunk leans back upon itself
Level with the earth, and sends out five
Feathery veins of branches on the sky.

I cannot stop and stare at her,
The wind cold, and I with work to do.
How can I stare at beauty?
It hurts.
There death leaves off, and love's hard edge begins.

MUSK

A touch of perfume upon her feet
To give them comfort and make them sweet,
Perfume also on either knee
And where her breasts part company
Perfume and reconcilement there;
Perfume atomized through her hair.

Who was little and full of guile,
Calculating to storm or smile,
Whole in happiness, deep in woe
Only a peace or two ago
Is now a woman with musk in her hair;
Power, and power's sweet sister, care,
Drift in a scented casual breeze
After her person, from her knees
And from her intimate, hinted places
Into the street and its staring faces.

Home Free

MUSIC IN THE AIR

What noise up there?
What but a duck in the moon-bright
Neck-sustaining air
Giving a quack to the night?

She makes the sky her pond and drowns the street
And drowns me too, homing on fishy feet
To where my doorway sucks its scaly mouth;
Heaven is north, and my drowned home is south,
And there my caverned coal fire covets me
Of the duck's night. Quack! in the dark, says she.

US TOGETHER

I do not like anything the way I
like you in your underwear I like you
and in your party clothes o my in your
party clothes and with nothing on at all
you do not need to wear a thing at all
for me to like you and you may talk or
not talk I like you either way nothing
makes me feel so nearly at home on Earth
as just to be with you and say nothing.

Home Free

US TOGETHER

I do not like anything the way I
like you in your underwear I like you
and in your party clothes o my in your
party clothes and with nothing on at all
you do not need to wear a thing at all
for me to like you and you may talk or
not talk I like you either way nothing
makes me feel so nearly at home on Earth
as just to be with you and say nothing.

Home Free

WINDY STREETS

Wind whirls the dust
    Into its nowhere, man dust and stone dust,
        And whirls the dusty news among the streets.
It is the old implacable enemy.

A man ages in the wind,
    Wears out his bravery,
        And the wind hounds him and gets at him,
Gathers his dust into its whirling nowhere.

Home Free

THE OLD MAN

It serves the old man right,
Right is what it serves him,
Coming out in the light,
    Out of his leafy dark,
If life's glare unnerves him.

Now he is cross and blind,
Light has left him blinded,
He gropes about to find
    The dark he came out of
But all darks are minded.

I know the poor old man,
Know him in my small heart;
I shun him when I can.
    Who chose for him? I ask.
His part is not my part.

Nevertheless I see
Him everywhere I look,
In me or out of me,
    His hunting, dazzled eyes
Give me back my own look.

Christ have mercy on me,
Forgive this mortal fear;
My five wits have drawn me
    Out, into the open,
And only you are near.

NO WAY OUT

No excuse
  Though I keep looking for one;
No use
  Pretending it is not me, has not been done.

No way out
  But always farther in
In doubt,
  Fate-strong, heart-struck, ground fine.

I have not
  Seen Paradise, nor its trees,
But what
  I glimpse of unspoiled brings me to my knees.

Home Free

AN AFFLUENT GRACE

I sit before my splendid thawed-out meal
And thank God for the hunger that I feel.
Grace before meat still speaks its firm amen:
Dear God I am luckier than most men.
My children are not hungry, maimed or lost,
By and large my ambitions are not crossed,
By and large I have good works yet to do
Being one of God's dwindling favoured few;
I can spare from my table, blest and crammed,
Thawed-out crumbs for God's multiplying damned.

THE HUNTRESS

The spider works across the wall
   And lo, she droppeth down!
The weather gathers in to fall
   And turns the garden brown.

Poor little spider, late astir,
   Disconsolate she weaves;
No creature comes to nourish her,
   Wherefore she hunts and grieves.

Home Free

THE BLESSED ANGEL

A blessed angel lighted at my window
– One of those I knew when I was born –
And, with his big wings fanning the air inward,
Studied me, but otherwise no motion.

It was a dark afternoon, I remember the clouds,
And a noise among the fields, empty and loud;
A noise in my own room, among the pictures,
And in the eyes of the angel, angel pity.

His careless glory overwhelmed the room.
How kindly had he come! He broke my weakness
And, in his kindness, put me back together.
Then off again to his tiny heaven flapped.

Home Free

BLISS

The less said about Edward's slut the better,
Nobody knows who she is or how he met her
With her waterfall of yellow-coloured hair
And feet like scissor points, a spiky pair.

Melancholy of love improves her lies,
Melancholy of gin makes deep her eyes,
Melancholy of streets refines her touch,
Sweet melancholy of tongue and teeth and such.

When summer evenings come across the tracks
We spread ourselves with beer and paperbacks;
Down comes Edward, powder on his face,
To take his slut out smooching every place.

Bliss is nice, but a little bit will do;
Edward has had too much, and his slut has too;
Only to see the hoof-marks in their eyes
And hear them wheeze would make a fellow wise.

HOME FREE

Someone has given Edward a pass to Paradise:
Take it, they said, and go; you'll never earn the price.
Walk right up to the dragon, keep an eye for the tree,
Show your pass to the angel and he'll admit you free.

Edward sweats for a fortnight, the salt is in his shoes.
Who knows about angels until he hears the news?
Who knows about gardens until he smells the pit?
Edward is holding a pass, and he's afraid of it.

Home Free

A NIGHT PIECE TO MRS. TREED

Treed around the corner,
     Treed in the park,
Treed among the potted palms,
     Treed after dark.

Never mind the garden its
     Nice beside the lake;
Rye bread and sausages
     Are the things to take.

Across the beaded water
     Twinkling with the cars,
Come to us upon the breeze
     Voices and guitars.

City noises rise and fall and
     Rise again and fall;
Strollers pass us by like gods
     Nor notice us at all.

Here amid the evening life
     By the lamplit shore,
Mrs. Treed, we're he and she:
     Who could ask for more?

BALLAD OF JARVIS STREET

As I was going down Jarvis Street,
  (Blow away the smog!)
A pretty Canuck I chanced to meet.
  (Rivers of sewage, down to the sea.)

I said, My girl, come give me a kiss,
  (Blow away, etc.)
And we'll marry and get the hell out of this.
  (Gallons of whatsit, etc.)

We'll take the Tube and suburban bus,
  (Roll out the tar!)
And live where no-one will notice us.
  (For the automobile is king of the land.)

We'll go where the trees are cleared away,
  (Bull-dozer country.)
And purchase our nest, and spend our pay.
  (Out where the blue comes down to the sprawl.)

We'll have our fun as Canadians do,
  (En Français, for a lark.)
Swimming and drinking and pitching woo.
  (Quelqueschoses sur les plages publiques.)

What do we do when it gets us down?
  (God bless our children!)
Re-locate in the heart of town.
  (And give us a tasteful country to live in!)

MULTITUDE

Of Sadie's bridal nights, the fruit
    Shine on the swarming earth
In their statistical exuberance,
    An exponential birth.

Largesse of Sadie's chiefest joy
    They populate the lots
And the best eating and drinking places
    Behaving like big shots.

Across the countryside their works
    Cover the stones and grass;
They hunt their multifarious purposes
    Amid the steel and glass.

They nurse their elbows and their knees;
    The smells of cooking fat
Hang about their sweaty doorways
    Where love puts out her mat.

Good night, my children's little children,
    Your mother's heart is blind;
She multiplies your hopes like vermin
    By way of being kind.

Home Free

LOVE IN HIGH PLACES

Always the same story,
    Too many bills to pay,
Telephone threatening disconnection
    And another baby on the way.

She lies like a bag of things
    On the bed
And schemes go round in circles
    Round and round in her head,
Many of them not good.

Beside her breathes her husband
    Her good man
Out of the urgent millions of whose middle
    She generated Dan
    And Mary Ann;

Likewise the urgent newcomer
    Inside
Drinking her blood and sorrow and
    Not satisfied,
    Kicking to get outside

Into the breathing world
    That his mother knows well
– Or her mother as the case may be –
She, the mother, knows all about it
– About the world, that is –
I mean, the mother of whoever it is knows all about the world
    And thinks it is a sell,
    More than three parts hell.

Some of the circling schemes
In her head
Have to do with the propinquity of her husband,
Whether him dead
Would be bad
Or just sad.

She thinks of some bright fields
Where they might go
And she under the bright sky clobber him
Lay him low,
Bury him,

And then set up a wailing,
Make the ground wet
With the bitter tears she would be shedding
Of regret,
Inconsolable
Regret.

Two o'clock in the morning:
Whoever Junior may be
Is bringing pressure to bear on her bladder;
Gets up to see
If Dan and Mary Ann are covered,
Ease the pressure.

God's image in the rooms,
    In each bed
A terrible burning fiery furnace
    And dreaming head,

And in Sadie the mother
    When she lies down again
A restlessness that will not let her sleep,
    Restless pain,
Discontent with her bone structure
    Worse than pain.

At last sleep overtakes her
    When dark turns grey
And the first merciless children's noises
    Greet the day:
Sleep for her weary brain and bone structure,
A little sleep
    Before the onset of day.

Sadie my only one love
    Sadie my bird
You have cause to be sorry for yourself
    Believe my word:

You have gone and loved yourself
    Into a trap,
Husband a good-natured good-for-nothing
    Unlucky chap;
If he would be a real bastard
You might give him up.

Let me tell you something about the
    Permissive land
Whose way in is through the medicine cupboard you
    Understand,
      Right at hand.

Home comes Edward in the evening
    To find her out
Cold on the chesterfield, Dan and Mary Ann
    Playing about;
Sleeping pills scattered on the floor
Dismay him,
    Plunge him in doubt.

Something in the situation causes him
    To not act,
Being alone in the room with the children
    And a big fact,

So that when he tried to do anything
    He shook,
Pick up the telephone or either
    The telephone book
Even just think of taking a grip and he
    Shook and shook.

In the region of his stomach
    The shakes begin
And work from there violently outward
    His knees and chin
Shaking most.

The children stop playing about
   As though they guess
An overriding catastrophic misery
   Which they express
In piercing and unpleasantly pitched noises
   Of distress.

These noises
   Come down the stairs
To Mrs. McGonigle's apartment where she conducts
   Her affairs.

She is a compassionate woman
   And up she goes
Upstairs, holding herself together,
   Because she knows
That these are not just the usual offended
   Or pounded noises.

There are occasions that a sentimental man
   Will not forget
But will look back upon with twinges of emotion
   And some regret,
When his behaviour has been as he thinks impulsive
   And warm and wet.

And he will also remember
   In his gut
Times when his yea should have been yea
   And it was yea but;
Perhaps his best friend hunted in the street
   And his door shut.

So Edward will remember
   This busy night
When Mrs. McGonigle hurried up the stairs
   And put things right
   And he went white
And wanted to help in the worst way but could not
   On account of fright.

And when Sadie was in hospital
   Tucked in bed
And Mrs. McGonigle back upstairs again,
   Children fed,
Cat put out
She did not go back to her smelly apartment
   But stayed instead
And slept with Edward.

Sadie my little true love,
   Sadie my bird
The peace you were almost granted
   Has been deferred.

I would excuse you from life
   If I could
But never mind, do not lose your nerve,
   Be good.

Edward really means well
   No doubt
But he keeps getting frightened off
   And found out;

No gift for happiness
   – How sad –
Nor for reliability either;
   Too bad,
Bad for you,
But do not give up.

After some clumsy months
   The baby is born
Nearly killing his mother in his emergence
   Leaving her worn,
Reeking of anaesthesia
   And torn.

A wind blew in from the arctic
   During the night
Making the weather of his first day
   Cold and bright.

When Edward saw the child
   He was afraid;
His knees and his lower jaw began shaking
   And he prayed,
He really prayed.

Somewhere, he prays, in Canada there must be
   Somewhere
Surely a pleasant, sheltered garden,
   Green and fair,
Maybe even way down in the city
   In its own air,

Where there would not be births or dreadful pain,
   And fun
Would have no exquisite hook inside it;
   What was done
   Would be done
And over with.

The child was named Stan
   To keep the rhyme,
A thing that parents forget about
   Half the time,
That names
   Can rhyme.

And when he grew up he was an earnest
   Successful man,
Earnest about Liberal politics,
   He ran
For Parliament and got in.

Up to Ottawa comes Sadie
    To keep a flat
For Stan and give parties for him,
Write speeches,
Meet women's clubs
    And all that;
    High-toned flat,
Nothing else but.

There is something Canadian
    About success;
Sadie felt quite at home with it,
    Stan no less.

And there is something Canadian
    About prayer;
Look for Stan and Sadie in church most Sundays
    And they are there.

Sadie put in a good word
    For Stan,
Hoped he might take his proper place
    In God's plan.

And in the comprehensiveness of her
    Mother's heart
She remembered Dan who had got off to
    A bad start
And Mary Ann who was a failure
    As a tart.

Sadie my boyhood sweetheart,
  Sadie my dove,
What do you suppose poor Edward's ghost
  Is dreaming of
  Now that his love
Has made its way into the government of the country?
Would he have guessed, that sentimental night,
  That his sweet shove
Would carry so far?

Stan grows more serious and thoughtful
  Day by day,
And serious people listen thoughtfully
  To what he has to say;
I am getting close to the truth, he observes,
  I am going the right way.

Something in his manner
  When he spoke,
Lack of confidence when he told a
  Sarcastic joke
Reminded Sadie of Edward and the dead years –
  Made her choke.

And she would think of how she loved her
  Successful son,
His helplessness partly, and the many splendid things
  He had done,
Their life in Ottawa
In its queer way
  Fun.

There was a little civil servant in the same
   Apartment block,
Stan was aware of her sometimes
   On his walk.
Then one day something happened,
They were on the elevator together
Just the two of them,
   Fell into talk
And Stan shook.

And he thought, It is no use, young woman
   To look my way.
You think I am a playboy, well, I have a
   Serious part to play,
No time for joy.

But then when he went to bed
   He knew he knew
That they would meet on the elevator again
And he would shake
Again,
   Nothing he could do.

He said to his mother,
   I love this land,
But sometimes when I think of its enormousness,
All its nature,
Its wastes,
   I do not understand.

I shall bury myself in committee work
   To ease the strain,
And attend to the complaints of my constituents,
   It will keep me sane.

Sadie my *raison d'être*
   I really hate
To be warning you about your child Stan
And your happiness here,
Especially now
   When it is too late.

But never mind, you can go over
   To Dan;
His life is a mess but he will do
For you
   What he can,
Being a soft touch
   Like his old man.

Of course you will not want to
   Give up success,
You have had so little of it in your life
And it is so sweet,
   Nevertheless
   You have had your share, I guess.

The little civil servant's name
   Was Gert;
She was so cute you knew she
   Must be dirt.

Love is like an insidious
    Mortal stain,
As though when you get it on
It goes deeper and deeper
    And you cant get it off again;
And it is like a rot
That itches
And scratches sweet
    And full of pain.

Dear Venus, evening star,
    Over the river,
You shine on Hull, your devout
    Pleasure-giver,
Its love lights winking and blinking.

Stan looked at you out of his office window
One spring evening
    And thought of Gert;
She had thrown a look at him over her shoulder
And it itched sweet
    And hurt.

Next thing they are together
    In Hull,
And Stan finds that his routine has changed from busy
To busier
    And far from dull.

There were times when his trouble would come back
    And he would shake:
A wistful evening when the urgency had gone off
And a warm breeze come on
    Beside a lake,
Gert there next him behaving like a delicious
Irrecoverable
    Mistake.

How can I be happy
    He wondered, or self-possessed,
When in fact most of the time I am anxious
    And depressed?
I see the love lights winking over the river
    That break my rest.

Yet he knows that he is happy
    In a way,
So happy, so full of himself and the world,
    So compassionate, so gay,
There must be sooner or later a terrible
    Big price to pay.

Stan and Gert found a place among the
    Pre-Cambrian rocks
Where they could go for week-ends and take off their
    Shoes and socks
And hats and coats and underwear and, well,
Find out about each other,
    And go on walks.

Earliest explorations
   Are not the best:
Scurvy, mutinous crews, uncharted waters
   And the rest;
Yet never again perhaps,
Never in the same way
Is the edge of the world just over the horizon,
   Sailing west.

Stan thought that Gert was the
   Innocent one;
Maybe so,
Though it would strain credulousness to believe it,
Yet in each there was a kind of virginity,
   Rather overdone
   That made for fun.

Sadie, there is something I did not
   Tell you about,
Which is that this poem has to do with love
Which is as much as to say
   Keep out
If you know what is good for you.

Yet I am glad you are in it
   Just the same;
Without you there would be little suffering,
Few regrets,
   No shame,
The whole thing would be tame.

Stan has always got his constituency
    On his mind,
Demands of his party, and his own special project,
The wilderness,
    So he can brainwash himself and leave behind
Shame, regrets, Gert's security-risk uncles,
Fellow-travelling boyfriends,
    Things of that kind

And also find time to relax with her in their
    Pre-Cambrian nest
And listen to her brushing her teeth
In the morning
Into the lake
Thinking, It is a good life:
    All is for the best.

He has great faith in life,
    He knows enough
To aim well within the ring of the possible,
Believe his promises,
Live with the threat of nuclear unpleasantness
    And yet be tough.

And when he grows tired of Gert
    As he will soon,
He will stay with her just the same
And play her over now and again
    Like an old tune,
Boring perhaps, but nostalgic.

He will have a career,
    Wont he just,
Being a man his party can
    Completely trust:
Wise, worried-looking, under a
    Diplomatic crust.

And dont think I dont mean wise
    Because I do;
You will be proud of him over and over
    Before you're through,
Even when you are all alone
    And cross, and blue.

For for the making of decisions there is also a
    Price to pay:
Promises, youthful idealism, private integrity,
Time for mother even
    Must give way
Before the harsh realities of this dangerous world
    As they say.

And Stan will be big enough
To pay the price
And some who preen themselves on their integrity
Will revile him
Not to his face exactly, but everywhere else,
    Nevertheless his advice
Will be sought by men we all respect,
And his public image will be
    Not really nice
But effective
Somehow.

And if you ask yourself where all this comes from
    And answer true
You will have to admit that his father contributed nothing
But good nature
    And a nervous tic or two.
His ability to stay afloat in a backwater of statistics
And swallow his pride
And speak bad French and get along with the French
And guess right about the United States,
And still be someone,
    Must have come from you.

BEDTIME

Edna the dog is dead and so is Min;
Mr. Smith's diet worked and now he's thin;
Walter has left the park for his loving wife:
Better warm than happy defines his life.

Toads are asleep and so are bugs and snakes;
Millions of things are asleep in the icy lakes;
Edward's asleep where brown stalks fuss and wave,
And a squirrel has planted oaks beside his grave.

Happy Enough

OUTDOORS

Everyone gone away
feasting but Nora, Mark
and me. Neither do we
stay put. It is getting dark

and on the horizon
the haze is grape-coloured;
an orange quarter moon,
under-ripe and pallid

lies in the murk down low;
the field ends are haunted.
I let myself go slow
while the two race ahead,

gleeful, inky leapers
in the warm gloom; I strain
to glimpse their dark capers
by the dusk of the moon.

Happy Enough

INDOORS

Says the window
   what heart
   in this weather?

Says the blizzard
   outdoors.

Says the pond
   slow blood
   deep down
   in hard mud.

Says the world
   no peace
   no shelter.

Says music
   the life.

Says the evening
   shut.

Says the stove
   hot iron
   hot breath
   in the pipes.

Good night.

Happy Enough

DEEP

My walls bend over me
and my dolls and my creatures;
there is frost on the window,
we hardly see out;

and quietly all night
    the snow,
dont feel it in my sleep
but deep down one flake after another
    deep.

Happy Enough

WINTER MAN

Snow nose
   head filled with snow
snow all down the front of his trousers

snow woes
   sleepy feelings of snow
hungry for snow supper.

Happy Enough

THE WRECKER

All gone still
    and queer,
over the fields a
    dark something.

Bed for me but
    not sleep,
not
    now I dont. Then

noise
    terribler
than thunder; I
    get brought down

stairs again
    in candle light,
everybody looks
    scared so I

sit close on my
    father's knee; it
howls out
    side like a

giant, it
    stamps
wants
    in.

Happy Enough

Shakes the earth, then
   gone,
nobody speaks;
   the house has been shaken

so we look around in
   doors and out,
trees broken, branches on the ground,
   water on the floors.

Soon neighbours
   to talk
stare and visit
   way late.

Next day
   chain saws;
that old
   sky grins.

SHADOWY

Endearing nakedness
that takes
at unawares
—how otherwise?—

bright
mortal
touched with darkness,
endeared by dark.

Happy Enough

SHADOWY

Endearing nakedness
that takes
at unawares
– how otherwise? –

bright
mortal
touched by darkness
endeared by dark.

Happy Enough

COLD JUNE RAIN

In
    for the day
what do we do in the rain?

Hear the news?

Listen to the old tunes?

Look, the sun
fleetingly on the floor
    a window shape
    dropped.

Happy Enough

1 Green leaves and
   stems that break
   out yellow all
   over the turf

   a sunniness im
   possible for a small
   girl not to pick
   and go on picking

   till it speaks
   golden speech
   throughout the downstairs
   wherever dark lurks.

2 Stone becomes no
   stone its face
   becomes no

   face but high
   in its cloud
   sea birds brood.

Happy Enough

3 Half-unheard over
head a mating

wing whir in the half-
dark late night

looming fells
and dales are still

we whisper
it is so still.

ONGOING

A green such a green o quivers
in a green sign across the street, I sit
at the customer's side of a desk, bargaining
for the least funeral. The undertaker
stalls, pondering my case.
We are in company with death, we two,
but the ongoing has its hook in us.

Happy Enough

THE STREET IN FALL

Apocalypse of leaves,
emerald, gold, blood colour;

the town all around me
and in my head;

I am stilled by the let-go
the stems give.

Happy Enough

OCTOBER SNOW

Wander down cold
flakes through clear air
spotting the space
between trees; windless, unmotivated
only for gravity and
its freaks.

My blood
keeps a strict
beat in the multitudinous
calm earthward of white.

CATPATH

Black on Mrs. Crowder's post
   watching
tabby on Mr. Moir's post
   watching
Mrs. Osborne's bullhead marmalade tom
footing along the catpath in the snow.

Happy Enough

OCTOBER

Day falters and the fields
lie reconciled. October.
The old man goes and sits

in the sun
under his maple
and feels the splendour on him.

His way into the dark
of dirt and stone:
through the blazing season.

Trusts it
as his beasts do
or the lit lamp his tree
struck by frost.

Happy Enough

LATE SPLENDOUR

We ought
    to have time for her;
somehow not.
    Nice, we say,

to see you out in the warmth,
    cant stay.
Oh, just for a minute for old
    sake's sake,

says she.
    If it would come for her
with a swoop
    while the dear sun shines.

Happy Enough

HAPPY ENOUGH

Happy enough
– empty-headed –
to the little field corner
building where

heifer
– eyeballs –
on the morning
sunlit concrete
and Fred

– face
lopsided
put clove stuff to it
didn't help none –

takes her and gently
brings her head down to the
gun she
drops he
opens her throat.

Get it fixed Fred it
hurts just knowing how it hurts.

Happy Enough

EUGENE THORNTON

Hours at sea we flew the metal
through equatorial weather, eyes
on the waters and their bunched ships;
    your key
    was our patrolling speech.

Destroying engines, landfalls, times of arrival,
comradeship of boredom, random postings,
drunk partings;
    day following day your wit
    comforted,

and you had your stratagems:
I remember a training night
and an aircraft no-one wanted to fly:
    duff wireless, you declared,
    and that was that.

After the war some letters,
photographs:
your one-year-old standing on your held-out hand.
    The gaps widened.
    Closed again –

all at once they are gone.
We meet at your bedside, your wit
still comforts, but your stratagems
are done.
    We yarn.
    It is not our first goodbye.

Happy Enough

F.H. UNDERHILL, 1889-1971

Who knows
by what right one is happy
   speaks wise,
honest and sharp-tongued to
   his world,
unhopeful that it may come
   unsnarled.

We saw
you small upon a platform
   yet so
that every corner quickened
   with what
your eye laid open and
   your wit;

   now gone;
our comfort, to remember
   a man
stubbornly the same, stubbornly
   himself;
public than private, no less
   himself

   and our
Frank, who marked, for all his
   candour
easier than we deserve. As
   we know
the last mark will be harder.
   Adieu.

Happy Enough

THRASH

The green we see
    from our kitchen:
Fred's oatfield,
    aging now, turning bronze.

His old thrashing mill
    gone to ground
hears of a sale:
    back home again with another old one.

All afternoon hammer the pulleys
    until they budge;
glum kind of an afternoon, cussed at,
    spoiling to rain.

Next fine day, coupled up,
    the jaws accept the proffered oat bundles
and thrash them, thrash, thrash, thrash,
    forked load after forked

load, what's left of summer.
    We lean against the truck, finger the grain
and drink Fred's apple wine
    for the truth in it.

Happy Enough

PRIDE OF OWNERSHIP

I was just out to look at the hives
from a suitable distance, after supper;
one bee comes right over and attacks me
and stings me. Does itself mortal damage.

On my wrist; my hand swelled
till it was like a blown-up rubber glove
and hurt; got into everything I did –
reading, fighting off sleep, talking to Jeanne.

Two days it was tight and hot,
then itchy; I can still feel it.
I shall take off that honeycomb
with gauntlet, veil and smoke, the full armour.

Happy Enough

A VISIT

Through mountains to the coast
at the machine's pace, faces
snatched past, towns, altitudes
rain curtains in the valleys; a sudden
snap of thunder, un-
reverberant, reminds us
that we are everywhere and nowhere
at home. The speeding sun. Your map,
four hundred miles of it
comes to its point at last
which is you
both,
the landfall of your roof.

The day winds down for us.

You take us to your shore, we
taste the sea. A smoky
sou'wester is blowing, the boats
click: townsmen's boats
and one lobster boat, and there is a lighthouse
lived in but no longer blinking,
aloof in the late sun,
sea-scoured and like the hour of the day
dusky.

Then indoors and the sacrament
of food. And talk,
words, treacherous vessels,
that bring us out from a few familiar landmarks
into vertiginous waters.

Happy Enough

We are committed to them, all
they are we are, we four
around your table, reaching into the night,
our lighted space like a boat;
outdoors the wind pushes
mindlessly, and a fleeting
star or two denote
the immensity our lamp makes small.

Inshore somewhere – where? –
the big world whines
its unimaginable threat.
Hard to believe in it here,
the bloody sweat,
but we do, we do not forget
the luck in our talk.

COMPANY OF THE DEAD

In lead and gumwood
   you came
   a long way home
your bitterness
abruptly
thugged out

   and we laid you
   under the bright
   October turf
   of your birthplace
awed that the Brute
had felled you.

   For your disdain?
   your innocence?

We spoke our words
of comfort
hoping to be excused
   – not by you
   whose pride
   was truth, truth pride.

A little sun,
   scud-broken
warmed us a little,
though not your undertaker:
   Hats on, said he,
   outdoors.
   One funeral at a time.

Happy Enough

Survivors
do not choose
among their dead
   whose sidelong eye
   will haunt them.

Among more beloved
your presence
lingers,
   your elegance
   and lurch.

   No staying power
   you said once,
   not for my ears, but I heard.
Outstayed you, though,
half a life
at cost
of knowing my dark.

I feel yet
the wrath
of your death,
   may envy its youth
   one day
but not now,
least now,
grown vulnerable
in my loves.

Nor shall I lay your ghost
   which I know
   as I did not you.

Happy Enough

WILD APPLES

Gone back to the wild
these apples

that round sour-skinned
out of their leafage.

Afternoon
unhurried

in dark heat
gnaws at them.

Happy Enough

NONSTOP JETFLIGHT TO HALIFAX

Never such comfort, annihilation
of the way there. But that's me! I
am the way there. These blandishments, these
knees and elbows bringing me food and drink
in high sunshine over high cloud

– to distract me.

Now that we're so far up why dont we stay?

Non-question of a non-questioner
as the stewardess knows, having
smiled on my effacement.
But she gives me a look.
Never mind, I say. Sit down
beside me. Perhaps on me.

BACK TO THE IRONBOUND SHORE

We smell it
coming back
   years on, late in the year
   and the day
   sea fog among the branches;
smell rock and tide,
the drowning that climbs and falls away.

Cove, open sea; the boat
clambers into the swell;
   we shout at one another
   groping out of the past:
   Harris dead, Percy crippled up,
   still out to the nets, though, him and young Paul.
Hull plunging;
our words against the exhaust.

Occulting light
narrows our void,
the foghorn corners the dark.
   We look for homelier rays;
   Purl's first, then Percy's, Isaac's, Charley's,
   the island bodes itself
   in their windows.

Happy Enough

In hollow light the winch
tugs us up the lanch:
    fish gut, fish liver, fish in brine,
    we know them,
    stink of salt muck
    among stones,
      the quick of the shore.
We follow the dark path
to Percy's.

The door opens into warmth.
    What body do we take to judgement?
    whitehaired, weathered, arthritic?
    sturdy, still gentler than one remembers,
    Percy between his canes, Eva watchful.
The room judges:
dont stay away so long
we may not be here next time.

Happy Enough

SELF PORTRAIT, GERALD TROTTIER

Studies himself in the glass
and what he paints he knows:
see, the pierced face,
the nostrils, eyes,
the line down between
and across.

Happy Enough

KNOWN

What's left
   of a long life
leaked into and out of:

   the wide
sky
   of your look.

Your web
   trembles
you know me.

   The times we had
father and son,
   the tunes you would whistle.

Happy Enough

THE COMMONWEALTH AIR TRAINING PLAN

Prairie birds in our training
   biplanes
over wheat acres all
   long summer ago;

poising the skyline we
   larked
spinning through turbulent air downwards,
   recovering;

war weather gods, toy
   thunders
hardly more airborne
   than grasshoppers.

Happy Enough

THEN OBLIQUE STROKE NOW

Whether as thugs, guns, the breaking of metal,
bursting, starving, smothering or long drawn out
in the gumshoe precincts of a hospital,
whether his frightened grin or his frightful pout,

I shall know him for my own with what little
spit I have left, after a lifetime lucky
cajoling him, my time now transcendental,
ready to grapple I trust as he with me.

Happy Enough

THE DAY THAT WOULD NEVER COME

The day that would never come comes, it is
not what was expected, not the dreamed of
gay trip to Montréal and the gay leave
taking on the dock for Europe for whose

conquest, making of many friends; she
no longer wants to go but she must,
nobody says so, but the last
thing she would do is turn back and I

think, That's my Peggy, which makes this a love
poem. Is there another kind? but is there
something else to be told, of the tremor
of the ship, the day's departure, her wave?

Happy Enough

CONVOCATION ADDRESS:
QUEEN'S UNIVERSITY, 29/5/71

Entered an urban scene
    by Lake Ontario
at home, at summer's end, 1913,
those years
when winter stilled the streets
and there were sleigh bells.
The world shifted gears.
    It seems long ago

but it was lo,
    yesterday,
and the between
    has ebbed away
as though it had never been,

and left me high
    on your shore
honoured by you, which I
    am humble for.

Your turn cometh
    in sight:
trust your luck,
dont kid yourselves that you dont
kid yourselves;
    live right.

Go forth, young woman, man,
    with your degree;
be lucky and happy as you can;
good advice
    you'll see.

Happy Enough

Find your own voice
   to tell
your story;
make good your choice
of the who and what with
   and tell it well.

True or untrue,
   tragic or absurd,
   your word
and how you say it
is you.

Hard words
   for our jaws
these days;
sacrifice
of a man;
our country
is not harmless as it used to seem to be –
   nor ever was.

Unforgivable,
   forgive,
we must know to the bottom –
the woe
and solace
   of how we live.

Happy Enough

Forth, I was told, go,
   near enough to the day
thirty-five years ago,
   a bright pm in May,
borrowed gowns and caps,
the girls carrying flowers,
are there generation gaps?
I thought so;
forth I went

to tell my story
   in my way,
no skipping,
no wanting to skip
so far
   I am lucky to say.

Yet scared enough
   God knows
of thundery stuff
on the sky-line;
what's coming
never looms
   in plain prose;

nor does the past
   stay put,
it rises up,
accusing ghost
   of what

and who
   we are:
half simple-hearted,
   half twisty, murderous, dire.

Just be happy
   in the sun
is our plea;
a small patch,
   our own fun,
no pangs;
   but we teach ourselves to be un-

or to get drunk
   or high
on drugs, booze, hard work, *la différence*
(lacquelle vive!)
not happy, not unhappy,
just drunk
   or high.

Yet some of us
   recognize
what it is when it comes
   in disguise;
we name its name
happy
and coax it.

Happy Enough

Best be let tangle
   in love's net,
and bid farewell
to liberty and all it has to sell
some time,
   perhaps not yet.

Connubiality, heavenly maid,
   descend,
we need you.
   Your strictnesses portend
   heartbreak in the end;
break us,
do not forsake us!

A cat crouched in snow
   contains its warm
hugged up
   in its cat form;
us not so,
we do not contain,
   and to keep warm
we hug one another;
cant go on hugging,
dont stay together,
hardly abide one another –
move over, cat!

What yarns, I wonder,
   will you spin?
Preposterous, beautiful, grandiloquent, sullen,
   uncorseted, laced in?

Happy Enough

Longer-winded
   than you expect,
with flourishes among the longueurs
   you would not predict,
and all dream-coloured somehow
   in retrospect.

Remembered tunes and odours
   from the years
will bring them flooding back
with a discomfort in the voice-box
   and tears.

Something we cannot do:
   speak plain
to the us that knows better
and sees through
   all we explain.
How we long to convince
this us, just once,
   and argue and plead in vain.

This morning, where is us?
   I am speaking to mine.
Do you hear me?
You think I am speaking to you,
who are you speaking to?
Do you say, This talk is very well
   or take some critical line,
and does your us agree?

Happy Enough

About us
    we only guess
in riddles:
our fates,
our telephone manners,
    unpryable-loose
as our smells,

our deaths –
    my death is a clown
the glimpses I have had,
with my nervous habits
    and my frown;
a not unamiable fraud
    but his jokes are low down,
and the company he keeps, dear God!

It all costs its worth
    no less:
what price failure,
    or success?
Love is very dear.
    Happiness,
unhappiness,
getting our own way
and so forth
cost the Earth.

But joy
    is free,
unasked-for, unexpected, undeserved
    as an honorary degree.
These are the last rhymes this morning
    from me.

Happy Enough

AGE

Peace, all but quite,
Jeanne talking to her cat
whose eyes are shut,
tail tip stopped, all but.

Pretend sleep
on an uncertain lap
with the familiar voice
quoting cat sense.

Age, that in its clutch
bears the spinal itch,
makes hind-quarters weak
and stomach sick,

also rounds the purr
rounder than ever before,
and brings pretend peace,
peaceful almost as peace.

Taking a Grip

Come out on deck.
The ferry heaved, and the islands

loomed in the rain.
We shall watch the puffins:

see, they forget where the wind is
and cant take off.

They scurry across the waves
on frantic wings.

My heart is aging,
yours is nearly fifteen;

you come in from dreams
and scurry with them.

Taking a Grip

BETWEEN

We are on a walk through fields
where Québec marches with New York
after tea, between Good Friday and Easter;
a warm, late afternoon, overcast.

The fields seem shut away
by a spell; elm, hardhack, wild apple
and the many kinds of thorn
bind their edges; here and there

an a-symmetrical, runt tree,
cobwebbed with vines, lifts, as I say,
in my Saturday afternoon vein,
beseeching arms. We are all three

witty. The walk is going well.
On to the ruined workshop under the willows,
with its gambrel roof and its clutter
of oak plugs, maple scantlings, butternut shells.

We peer into the farm living room
at the doll, still on the floor where the stove was.
The house is subsiding among raspberry canes
and box elders. The barn has at last caved in.

Hazy with new green and pink, the growth
offers no umbrage yet, only beneath
hemlock stands, in Fred's pasture and on the slope
back to the brook. We have a goal

Taking a Grip

which is to look at a black cherry tree
that Andrew knows. An hour and there it is
in a field fence beside a glade,
a strand of barbed wire running through it:

old black wire at the heart of an old black tree
whose bark curls and whose hard branches reach out
every way. We take our knives
to some lopped pieces and try them for the

dark grain of the wood. At this standstill
harmlessness becomes imaginable;
yet who can believe himself harmless, or herself,
even for a moment? We have come

roundabout and are now on our way home,
where gin and dry vermouth await us,
a good dinner and good company,
Sydney and Betty and us all.

But in this warm early dusk we are
spellbound, as though shut away from all that, no
mutability any more, no ties,
no crucified yesterday, no risen tomorrow.

Upstream. The low sun breaks cloud
as we come in sight. Mark runs, he dwindles
before our pace from which hurry
has been put by.

Taking a Grip

DAISIES

Stars
in a pastoral heaven;

eyes
with a queen's look;

fiat mihi
in petals;

Mary's flowers
bosomed among the grasses.

Taking a Grip

ANDREW PLAYS THE B-FLAT SONATA

Easy come   spring
new snow goes   in a dream
old snow lurks   dark
under the edges   darkens out around;
cold air warm sun   uncover old
hurts   over again.

What wants   to be said
so as to wake   Heaven
gets hardly   murmured
under the sky   words

between whom?   eyes
look up   a voice
breaks   recovers
and for a moment   we know one another,

as we know   Schubert
phrase by phrase   know
his cadences   tunes
out of my misery   he said;
hurt of thought   searched,
his longing   his
undernote   of thunder.

The death we owe   darkens
as his did   as winter
darkens   into spring.

Taking a Grip

LUCK

Bad luck to see the new moon
first through glass; I do
almost anything to be outdoors
when her cheek shows.

Good luck, I see her first
from the quay at Finbackfirth;
and not again till the night dawn over Tórshavn
turning her cheek away.

Taking a Grip

WHISKERY

Wind sounds
in the bare
branches, each
tree its own
note.

By starlight
see
whiskery
twigs among which
the wind
buzzes.

Taking a Grip

WINTERING

Wrapped
in tarpaper, tentest and styrofoam
they hold for spring.

On warm days they rid the hive of dead
and breed renewal. Some fly out.

Put your ear to the hole.
Between gusts you can hear them,
a bunched hum.

Taking a Grip

IN SPATE

Another winter done, brooks
    go shouldering through the fields
    with their icy trash.

Among the trees
    they hurry past one's eye.

No pools to brood in, flat
    water where it is low.

Roads get hurt.
    Fields dont show much hurt.

Taking a Grip

STRAWSMOKE

I begin to see fields
as a late-playing child
sees bed.

Dusky games are hardest
to quit.

They burn straw in the fields.
I wonder if I may choose
to burn.

Strawsmoke hangs
in curtains
against the twilight.

Taking a Grip

THERE

One keeps itching to get there. Where? Never mind
where; one gets there at last, and does not come back
again to tell anyone else where
or how, or what it is like there.

One drives internal combustion vehicles
or one walks, or one rockets across the sky.
Restlessness is the ness one goes by.
It infallibly takes one there.

Taking a Grip

BEING WAITED ON

I do not travel
but I think of the Jews,

am not waited on
without thinking of them.

What right have I to such thoughts
having been spared?

Dear God, I would spare my children
thoughts.

Taking a Grip

WHO BOMB?

Though I hate
my blood-drinking me
am not let forget
or disown him.

Broker of child-burning
sister-pimping
grows rich,
richer.

Safety of my innocents
is his concern,
pity
of our death.

My fear's lover
decider;
our both ache –
to be hid.

Taking a Grip

THE MARAUDER

First light,
turn for one last sleep.
The White Rooster sounded and I
   remember
   the trap.

Bed warm bed clothes and boots
   down to the barn
   with the gun;
maybe he wont be there,

but there he was
   in the corner
   egg and fowl crammed
   eyeing me back;
between us

an irrecoverable
   choice.

Taking a Grip

RIBS, ROASTS, CHOPS, BACON

Two pigs in straw
on the truck box floor
we have come to deal with you
in the way of our law,
survival, we call it.
Being under it too,
the beauty of its sternness,
beauty and dismay grown fast together,
we share the ruth
of this meeting.

By one hind hoof you are lifted
into an attitude that you detest,
heads down, throats addressed
to our thin blade
that first parts your fat
then thrusts into your jugular;
at once your blood comes bright
and your despair gores the air,
your death hangs.
A roaring flower of flame
refines your surface;
scraped down, scrubbed down, opened, emptied,
your organs are kept,
your bled flesh, divided acceptably,
wrapped and consigned to frost.

Taking a Grip

Some time friends come, or maybe
sons and daughters, and our mood
expands.
You have been fetched from frost
in one of your parcels,
your offering gratifies our feast
with its mortal savour;
we meet again, and our moment
is jovial.

Taking a Grip

SHORT UNTITLED UNCONNECTED POEMS

Wheel tracks to the fence corner
among the abandoned; a wet-ended afternoon
not far from home; the half grassed-over
chrome and shatter glisten at us.

    * * *

Wet-sheeted ice
ducks on it
wet-footed

repeated

    * * *

Rain, rain all night; the phone
wakes us. Wrong number. Fresh
wood on the fires, then back,
thankful, for a visit,
maybe a bit more sleep
in the dark before day.

Taking a Grip

DELAY

The pasture is cropped smooth.

Fred, Bob and I took off the honey; Mark too.
Three hundred pounds of amber, not to remember
earlier basswood and clover.

The garden yields its not
unqualified foison. Some surprises.

Crows are up from the trees.

It seems a time to be wishing one hardly knows what.

For the dead to come back? Not that.

For friends to be nearer?
Tempting, but not that either;
friends are where they are,
with visits and letters.

For release from longing?
Come, that is no wish
but weariness of the heart.

Crickets and katydids
tell delay in the fields
as though it will never end.

Taking a Grip

FOR GORDON AND HELEN ROPER:
TRENT UNIVERSITY, MARCH 6, 1976

The Good Lord looked on
Peterborough, that
rivery city
sixty-five years
ago; right spot
opined he, or perhaps
she, for a Canadian
bookworm: wintry
winters, indolent
streetlit summers
and the Great North, meaning
in that dawn, pre-Cambrian
rock slopes, and pastures
underfoot; favourite
Stoney Lake, book lake,
armloads of books, book talk
late into the loony
lakeland darkness.

Gorgeous books, how we
gobbled them, un-
troubled, undis-
mayed, not groping
either after
recondite meanings,
mere book-addicts.

Taking a Grip

The sweet hectic
fever, love, then
enters with his
wonders not kenned
in book-addiction;
distanced, alas,
the two lamps held
of study and nursing
in endured division,
Chicago, Toronto:
given and honoured
loyalty on which
marriage builds
a lasting fabric;
so too, teaching,
learning's largesse.

War interrupts
the first married
years in Carl Sandburg's
pork metropolis
and coaxes back
the nurse and scholar
back to our busy,
blustery, belittling,
strungout, yet somehow
homey Northland.

Taking a Grip

Then, the war over,
teaching again
in Trinity's Tudor
gothic corridors,
don and critic, homebody as well,
enviable at home,
friendly at work,
patient, even-paced,
thoughtful, responsive.
Slowly, whimsical
Fame befriends him
hard at his work,
not minding Her.

Life is longer
than we expect,
then all at once
it is no longer long;
children grown up,
students dispersed,
affection's circle
widening and widening;
beloved prof
a string of stories
larger than life,
a legend already
that does us good.

Taking a Grip

A LETTER TO MUNRO BEATTIE ON HIS RETIREMENT

Dear Munro,
                    It is twenty-seven years since I
under the eye
of A.S.P. Woodhouse
marched past in your march past,
and with the blessing of Northrop Frye
    you took me on
    and I took you on
    and presently we took Gordon on
and we three and Dorothy
took on the whole of Eng Lit
    from where it began
to T.S. Eliot
    with a touch of Am and Can
    and Dylan Thomas.
Water under the bridge;
it is time to speak of it
and where it ran:
    of the old building
    where everyone knew everyone
    and the talk all was
    of the wilderness
    that was to be the new campus.

There were occasions too:
when we went to meet Roy Campbell,
that self-styled bugaboo,
    we three
    wondering what we might see.
What we encountered was a thirsty man,
a farmer with a burly point of view
and epic talk.

Remember the cake you baked
with the inexplicable
big hole in the middle
which you filled full
of chocolate icing? That was a cake!

Happy waters under a happy bridge,
   or so they seemed
   for all their teaching load
   and un-negotiated wage.
Now comes the augmentation:
Rob and Mike first;
and then the great migration
to two and a half half-finished buildings
amid mud, din of construction, winter's rage.

There was a hanged man among the trees
   when we moved,
   an ominous find,
   we had left something behind:
henceforth our luck was streaked.
   We swelled our ranks
by twos and threes and multiples of threes,
   and rose between our banks
until, as the saying is, we peaked.

Taking a Grip

Waters are not so clear
as they seemed once;
troubles have mingled since:
deaths, griefs, grievances,
partings and disappointments;
bitter and cruel blows
struck your ebullience;
embitter you they did not
but they brought the eternal note
of sadness in.

Dear Munro,
Departments come and go
as we do.
Change does not pretend
to be kind.
Never mind, we have had a good run
with you;
more happy times than un-
and now this old-fashioned bit of fun,
a Beattie party
to wind down on.

Taking a Grip

KENT DOE'S ORDINATION

Keep your word is not
easy, without grace
not possible. I
trust your word, then, Kent.

Do trust all your words
outsize though they seem
even as you seem.

After your ordi-
nation came at a
dark time when I was

homesick in the world
I wrote about it
something comforted:

Now you are a priest
always, your old word
new given and kept.

Taking a Grip

G.W. & G.J. EXCHANGE EXAMPLES OF
THEIR CALLIGRAPHY – A CHINESE PAINTING

Gesture of exchange
    as though among the gorges
    where all seems menace
lights up our meeting
    graciously.

Your genius
for the precise
    informs your page
across whose surface
    what follows
    from your pen
    elegantly
makes elegant our sojourn
under these towering sublimities.

Taking a Grip

THE LANGFORD BAND

Look to, says Kay, treble's going,
   she's gone.
So campanology
   breaks out over Langford Village,
a jocund din that carries
   as the wind is blowing.

Chris listens
   and when the rounds
are striking evenly
   he grins:
Go Grandsire Doubles, says he,
   and then the fun begins:
Sarah goes down to lead,
   Janice makes thirds,
Andrew finishes dodging five four down,
   Tim lays two at the back
and the covering tenor bell
   is rung by Duncan Brown.

Bob! says Chris, with a grunt.
   Everyone changes tack;
Sarah comes out of the hunt
   and double dodges with Janice at the back;
Tim makes thirds and Andrew makes backwards thirds
   while Duncan rings right on;
he is a man of few words.

Single! is the next command.
Everything is going so well
    it could go on to a peal
but two hundred and forty is enough.
    And if Peter and Terry come,
those wizards in the land,
    they will have news to tell,
says Chris,
    that we've got a Grandsire Band.

Taking a Grip

APHRODITE

Rising
from my

inner
ocean

thoughtful
sometimes

or at
my books

your goddess
touches

where death
and life touch.

Taking a Grip

TALK

Harnessed catastrophe
   hurls you
   into our landscape
for a slow-lived moment

out along the brook
into the fields
   field talk
   brook talk

   and home again by the pond
pond talk

talk through whisky and the evening
   into our stillness
   late contentments, old
long since among us.

Taking a Grip

PEN Y MAES

Up the steep meadow
   as we best can
against the wind's rage
   on wet terrain
   fighting our way

to greetings,
reunion greetings
   and hot soup.
On its blustery hillside
your cottage
   seems wind-bludgeoned
   since winds began.

   Out into it is our plan,
   up the slopes,
what else?
   for us brief sojourners
   gone so soon
from these wild hill paths
and becks.

Evening swells to a feast
that hardly needs
   the edge that wine puts on
   or the elan
of candle-shine
to crown the day.

Afterwards, replete
   beside the fire
we read what Kilvert tells
   whose feet
   walked these roads
a hundred years ago;
   his curtal span
   and sage compassion
reach us:
   we have our stories too
and they are short.

White-eyed moon
   draws us forth again
   up Llanthony Hill,
   its moon-bare top.
Eastward the English fields
   and lights;
westward the priory ruins:
   man's work,
   age on age of work.

Dear John, Ann, Katherine, Mark, Benjy,
   they were our Welsh three days
   with you
   so quickly by
   and into our stories;
love, Mark, Nora, Jeanne, George.

Taking a Grip

COME, BOB AND NORA

Come for a visit,
a year-end feast;
old friends may join us,
old foes may too
stray from the shadows
that shape our myth;
wordless they ponder
our words that body them
forth from their left-off
fates into ours,
into our day's luck,
its dreads and longings,
its brightnesses
burgeoning as now
in white weather,
wood heat indoors.

Stoves make talky
centres for us,
reminiscence
rising and wandering,
ravelling the web
of former moods,
of half-forgotten,
half lived-over
evenings like these;
knitting up new
of known gestures,
of words with our own
histories in them.

Taking a Grip

Histories or myths?
Made or suffered?
Something of both
we seem to know
works the fabric
of staid friendship
weaving in threads
from war, homecoming,
homey decades
work-filled, festive,
fraught with children
and old loyalties,
those Earth fibres
aging to gold.

Taking a Grip

FUEL

Mindful of stoves in mid-August I become
owner of a chain saw; then off we go,
Fred, Mark and I, in Fred's tractor and wagon
and truck, to Highway Fifty-two

where they took out timber by the church
and ruined the bush road. Maple branches
in the dirt there, and lengths of beech and birch
since March. The front-end loader wrenches out

what's good, not cross-grained. In the church wall
under the window is honey; some ash
near by, but the bees are ugly; we leave well
enough alone and get down to work. Gnash

go the saws and puff blue smoke, teeth filed
to bite for us. If they bite dirt they must
be filed again. Cars pass on the road
going somewhere in haste. No haste

for us, ours is the wood's pace, fibrous.
And we are sociable: Jimmy Massey
visits us with his wisdom. The day wears,
the sun bears down; Mark loads and we

steam with sweat. There is pleasure in the wood:
under the axe it parts with an inviting
knock. We knock and knock; then Fred
consults his watch and the day ends. Bring

winter now. Bring cold.

Taking a Grip

Daylight and fields behind us we
enter the maelstrom; Aeroport
it keeps urging, and we comply
at speed, and out we come; arrivals

howl in overhead. I drop you
and Sue where it says Departures,
park and make my way back
to find you. Faces

from every corner of the Earth.
We are known, not a hair of our heads not
numbered, our meetings and partings
wept with. Some have destinations.

I think we are being formed up
for the Destination, that
is what these closed-circuit television
screens mean: the risen dead

are programmed. My heart sinks.
But then I find you, you
have a destination, your
baggage is being weighed, it is not

Doomsday after all, just au revoir.
You are excited, cant eat cake;
Sue and I can, though my heart
has floated up again into my throat.

Taking a Grip

If there could be no danger, no
more goodbyes –
I want to say yes but know
better; would not have you not

go, not take your excitement
through the gates to those
wings waiting
with their vehicular fires.

Taking a Grip

BOB TAKES A GRIP

The cesspit seems to be plugged again.
It wearies me to think of all that soap
and stones and mud. If only the drain
would be plunged and stay clear. What a hope!

Along come you on a visit.
What needs to be done? Well, the cess-
pit needs digging. But never mind it.
There you are in the morning, nevertheless,

up to your knees already. Heat.
And slime. I take a shovel
and by noon we have got it beat.
A new kind of pit, a dug hovel

with plank sides and a tin roof sodded over.
We admire what we have done.
This pit, we think, may last forever.
A beer, then, on the verandah, out of the sun,

and lunch to look forward to.
The drain taste will go
and before it does, with the help of this home brew
we shall forget it anyhow.

Taking a Grip

REMEMBERING MARGARET

March upstairs to be
   scrubbed
   regardless of fret.

More, though, I hark back
to your lap
that breathed of kind, my
   head in it
   stroked
   saying my prayers
the garden yet near by.

   Remote now,
having argued myself out
   where fears are
   and loves met.

Many an after supper
around the debris
unguarded
   laughing so, our
   cheeks wet.

   Missed
by a far chance
   your goodbye
   when your star set.

Stories you would like, I
keep meeting them;
   come back one after supper
   swap stories again
   Margaret.

Taking a Grip

GOODBYE, MARGARET

It turns out to be, as how
    could we know, our last walk
and talk together. Sun thaw
    made lacy the wrack

of winter in the streets.
    He is beautiful, you say.
I know that defeats
    are beautiful. One day

we come to our beauty,
    terrified or serene
or beyond both, more likely,
    knowing even as also we are known.

I guess I shall not again
    see him, as we leave his room;
his wits are gone
    and he is as though at home

yonder. He smiles from a distance;
    and he is, as you say, beautiful
for all his ambience
    of tubes and bottles, the whole

apparatus of delay
    that keeps some good things on,
his courtesy, and the play
    of his Irish sense of fun

but draws the rest out fine.
    You were not reconciled to age,
you hated the caving-in
    of your nerve, yet you stood at the edge

of his bed and smiled at him
    who had shared most of your life
and for whom you had become
    dim, and as if

with your first and last words blessed
    the old man. I think back
beyond much that is lost
    to the blessedness of your look.

It hardly seems a goodbye
    with you; not like the one
when I asked you not to cry
    and you hung on and hung on,

then broke at the last:
    a station platform, so
long ago in the past;
    vivid before me now.

Taking a Grip

You held your feelings there;
    at home they gave
my childhood its weather;
    you were not afraid to grieve

or to enjoy a good laugh,
    having both kinds of tears
and strong views enough,
    unbudgeable scunners,

loyalties like glue.
    What became of them all?
Sometimes I wish I knew.
    Dear God, perhaps I shall.

Sometimes I wish that I
    might have seen you once more.
What for, to say goodbye?
    Hard to be sure what for:

a hug,
    another gossip
this side of the big
    summing up?

Yet I cant not be glad
    that when you were sent for
and your days were yet good,
nights not yet bad
    you went.

Taking a Grip

There is a letter from Andrew
    on the table; it does not
look fatter than a page or two:
    let us open it and read it.

News, he says, first off. Kate and I
    have decided to get married.
Well, that is news! Good thing that we
    are seated, so as not to be carried

away, or knocked off balance, or what-
    ever. One begins to need a chair
for such news, and a pot
    of tea, and air.

What else does he have to say?
    Ordinary things, calmly told.
But we are not fooled; until the day
    the days between will be filled

with mystery and drama, the stuff
    of life. And now the day has come
and here we all are; it is enough
    to make the theme of a half-rhymed poem

this joining of two fates in one
    extraordinary one, not
bound at the edges but grown
    together, so that where they meet

there is both hurt and sweetness. We join
   in the making of this fate;
marriage is not just for one
   out of two; we are all in it

and our cue is, rejoice!
   We are invited by the future
and we respond, in a less equivocal voice
   than its, to this adventure.

Taking a Grip

TO BOB McRAE ON READING HIS BOOK:
Leibniz: Perception, Apperception and Thought

I have your book in hand.
   It awes me.
I used to understand
   epistemology

and feel somewhat at home
   among such things
as *cogito ergo sum*
   and its questionings.

Perception, apperception, thought,
   in Leibniz: imagine
bearing down on that lot
   with a rhyming brain!

Well, I bear down,
   exulting no little
over each dawn
   of intellectual

light that breaks over my earth
   (a metaphor
for what it's worth
   I can make more).

One difficulty is
   I keep looking up
the same words; entelechies
   was a stopper.

Taking a Grip

The dictionary reads
  in Leibniz' system
a word for monads;
    but I dont understand them.

I guess what they are
    and admire their spunk
after the Thirty Years' War
    to think

and apperceive and perceive
    and express, as Leibniz puts it,
what the world has to give.
    There is surely spunk in that.

Where he sounded words
    and you read his chart
I have been groping towards
    in my art.

That language is a mode
    of being rhyme shows,
but not being itself, God
    alone thinks what that is.

Awesome thoughts
    awesomely thought out.
Your prose begets
a rational pleasure
    that nobbles the old doubt.

FAREWELL TO TEACHING

Knowing what I now know
would I have consented
to be born? Next question.
When it comes time to go
will I go forlorn or
contented? Ask again.
Anything in between
should be easier. O
K, what made up my mind
to come to Carleton? Work.
My kind of work was not
easy to come by, I
came by it at Carleton;
it was simple as that
and lucky, plain lucky.
I cannot account for luck
but I can be grateful.
What was my kind of work?
Presumably teaching,
whatever that may be.
Teaching is a kind of
learning, much like loving,
mutual goings-on,
both doing each to each;
mutual forbearance;
life itself, you might say.
Whatever teaching is
did I enjoy it? Yes.

Am I glad to leave it?
Even of life itself
enough is enough. Good-
bye Dow's Lake, goodbye Tower,
essays, papers, exams,
you I can bear to leave.
But how shall I improve
the swiftly-dimming hour?
I shall deteriorate
amid bucolic dreams
and gather in my fate;
there's lots worse ways than that.

Goodbye good friends. Alas,
some goodbyes are like death;
they bring the heart to earth
and teach it how to die.
Earth, here we come again,
we're going out to grass.
Think of us now and then,
we'll think of you. Goodbye.

CONVOCATION ADDRESS
CARLETON UNIVERSITY, JUNE 4, 1979

Fellow graduates,
not many of you
have taken so long
to get here;
thirty years ago,
take away a year,
my labours began
at Carleton.
Now what do I know?
Not much about me,
by what right lucky
and fearful-happy;
not much about us,
learned and perplexed;
nothing about what next.
Otherwise enough
to get on with.
I know that I learned;
do not know that I taught –
maybe, maybe not.
I think we only learn
what is already there
in the grain.
Let us say we all learned.
For instance, I found out
something I always knew
about grades –
recovered knowledge
feels hard-earned.

Thirty years ago,
take away one,
honour, pass or fail
seemed weighty matters.
No longer so.
That was then.
Outlived all that,
out of school again.

Some of you have sat
and cerebrated with me,
taken notes, yet;
now I wonder what
you may remember
when you have careers,
affairs, families,
fetters of that sort,
will our thought
and learning together
give comfort
or make strange?

What did we not do
in the years, that they
became history
in that headlong way,
gone before we knew?

Nothing gets begun
but finds its time
and its look
and gets done;
the dearest moments
touch and are gone,
leaving thumb-prints.

Now is a moment
of the dear kind;
long-winded you say,
but never mind,
it will not stay;
already, see, it
is turning away,
tired of us,
going for good.
We have felt its eye
upon us,
its print is in us;
we would not hold it
if we could.
Goodbye moment.
Goodbye thirty years,
take away one.
Goodbye.

VENICE WITH BILL

Dear Bill, what one remembers:
the aurum we almost had,
we three in that arboreal
ristorante with the tree
growing inside, and two cats
playing among its branches.
Rainy and windy all day
at a time of high tides. You
spoke the words *acqua alta*.
Venice is slowly sinking,
you said. But we sally forth
after a day of splendours
to eat a splendid supper
and top it with an aurum. No
aurum says the waitress; she
points to a drain in the floor.
Up comes an inch of water,
then down again. We pay her
and say our goodbyes. Up comes
the water again to stay.
Outdoors the walks are awash,
ankle deep in some places.
Back at the pensione
water all over the floor,
carpet rolled up and away.

Our long-planned Venice meeting
is now in the past; sea-bright
it shines in our memories,
yet keenlier endearing Earth.
But when we come together
what is it we talk about?
Rum what the mind remembers:
the tree-filled ristorante,
cats playing in its branches,
home through *acqua alta,* that
aurum we never did have.

TED AND JENNIFER'S OKAY SITUATION

Okay situation
you say; a pronouncement
to be rejoiced in. Come,
you say. Something else. Not
every invitation
offers a trouble spot
pronounceable okay.
MIDDLE EAST AIR air me
oversea to Beirut.
Torn city. I enter
anarchy ages deep,
unresolvable strife
stubborn as the beauty
of Roman stone or steep
grove: Phoenician timber.
We drive past refugee
corrugated iron
and rubble. New trouble.
Your welcome comprehends
it all, old and new, life
that bides its history
and risk.

      Byblos, Baalbek –
old, unhappy, far-off –
you take me to see them,
unearthed and put on show,
in their disdain and wreck,
for whom? Us latecomers?
What awesomenesses here?
What worship, sweet with blood
under these Roman liths?

What gods in the sun-glare
lifted their skirts to go
leaving what earth-veined myths?

Back through the bountiful
Bekaa, through armed road-blocks,
back the Damascus Road
to your apartment. Guns
on the roof-top and ground
floor eye your day-by-day
that meets the Middle East
with aplomb.

              My brief stay
still holds a walk through town
through shot-pocked precincts, bright
with morning trade and sun
and our talk. We resist
lugubriousness, grateful
for this meeting of friends:
a gift, what else? Who knows
what all Beirut portends?

MIDDLE EAST AIR again.
Our gods are vehicular,
they eat space. Do not pray
to them, they are deaf; on
their way out already.

ROB'S LEISURE

Remembering a life well spent,
often harsh, whiles dangerous,
bears away old discontent,
evens out peaks of distress,
renders the stalwart heart wise
to view with charitable eyes.

May Rob, whose course has been such,
come to his leisure again,
dear-bought, therefore valued much,
offering good hours to the pen
unto whose haughty demands
gray matter strives to make fit
answer, from heart and with hands:
learned, most learned, and yet
lightly so, salted with wit.

FRED'S SIXTY-FIFTH BIRTHDAY

Who wants to reach
the venerable age,
who wants to age at all?
Give it up, Fred!
Twenty years ago
we encountered you
a strapping farmer
and fiddler
with a youthful wife
and four-year-old daughter.
Mounted on a new
Massey-Ferguson
you made fields and woods
machines and beasts
do as you told them to.
Think back, now:
hay
baled and put away,
munched and spread again;
stooked oats thrashed,
apples picked,
apples made into wine,
elderblow and stone-pile
grapes made into wine
to jollify the haying
and the haying barbecue.
Cows milked, think,
heifers bred and milked,
registered calves born,
beef, poultry, pork
and lamb put down to freeze.

Think of barn eggs
all over the place,
and cage eggs, and bees,
generations of them
swarming in trees
and shrubs; and the honey,
the honey:
day after day in the bee-house
uncapping and cranking
the old extractor crank.

Great deeds done
get thought back on
and told
to children
and grandchildren
who do their deeds
in their time
with some of our
cussedness in them.

SO LONG, ALBERT

Anyone in the know
at the Faculty Club bar
knows whose is the white
head among the great
gathered for a bite
and something temperate;
knows whose is the wit
that makes the table roar,
or pay attention when
he quotes Sam Johnson
giving chapter and verse,
or Charles Dickens, or the Bard,
a catholic, copious choice
among the great and memorable,
to sound in his bardic voice.
Anyone can see
that he is a great man
able to speak the word,
and look it, and mean it,
sing it, if need be,
as who else can?
Loyal colleague, friend,
father and husband,
a most companionable
man, humble withal,
too much so to admit
his own humility.

Greatness comes among,
befriends and goes again
as we know it must do;
nothing we love stays put,
nor should we want it to;
meetings, partings, the waters
close over and heal
in their unthinking way –
but thinking is what matters;
unhealed is our privilege,
the high price we pay.
So long, Albert, alias
Bud, we'll think of you,
we'll keep the wound open
as you will do for us.

A CELEBRATION FOR NORTHROP FRYE,
MAY 28, 1980

Moncton, did you know
that in your streets grew
    Canada's famousest
    speed typist,

and that his childish fare
included Samuel Butler
    at your Maritime
    bosom

and Bernard Shaw? Two such
master wits would teach
    his wit
    to bite.

Where earlier might he
than at your riparian knee
    glimpse fame
    first infirm-

ity as well as last
of noble mind? West
    ward Fame
    beckons him

and there Toronto won
his affection
    and held it,
    holds it yet.

Victoria College gave
him connubial love:
    Helen,
    his emanation.

Emmanuel College coaxed
the preacher in him next,
    head stored
    already with the Word.

He reads THE GOLDEN BOUGH
and Spengler on the how
    of Doom's
    to's and from's.

But they very soon took
a back seat to Blake
    whose key
    lay ready

to unlock the door
on myth and metaphor:
    twin guides,
    true lodes

whereby to steer aright
thorough the seas of thought,
    their isles
    and perils.

Tribute to his guru
comes FEARFUL SYMMETRY,
 the clue
 to draw

Blake himself through his maze,
and us too, otherwise
 uninitiated,
 square-witted.

Followeth presently
the great ANATOMY,
 fourth level,
 anagogical,

whose pet word, genre,
became a shop-talk winner;
 pronounced jong,
 to rhyme with gong.

Fame, that busy one,
now lets him sit alone
 in quiet
 no whit.

Her delight is in Frye
cutting the airy way,
 his critical path
 around the Earth.

From all corners of the globe
the academic tribe
   lay claim
   to his time

already claimed at home
by class-room and board-room,
   Principal's chair
   and chore.

Ottawa likewise
enlists his expertise,
   much needed
   it should be said.

Amid all these labours
postwar Canadian verse
   proffers the burden
   of its bush garden

and he accepts, yet so
as to not stint the flow
   from his pen,
   a learned rain

of books, in which the whole
of thought comes to his call:
   man's art
   and his fate.

Now he circles back
to his great book on THE BOOK:
   his magnum
    opus to come.

There is room in his work,
the spirit ranges wide
   and meets
    not limits

but everywhere form,
imagination's home
   and hearth
    on Earth.

How do we honour one
already in the fane
   of honour,
    how bear

our messages of praise
before his critic's eyes?
   Well, anyhow,
    we do

confident of his smile
and knowing that we dwell
   this hour
    together
    in Eden's bower.

ODE

Composed for James Downey's installation as
President of the University of New Brunswick
October 16, 1980

Come the vision that on Mount
Patmos blazed; come event!
   But haste
   not, come first

festive days when we give
our dusty selves leave
   to cower
   elsewhere

while our glad selves deck
in silks and rhetoric
   some high
   solemnity.

With garlanding and bays
today we solemnize
   James Downey's up
   ward step

to heights whence he must sound
trouble's learned mind
   in Academe's
   domes.

Trouble comes the same
inland or maritime,
   dried out
   or wet

and they whose gift it is
to sift cross purposes
   and make
   them speak

as though in harmony,
God speed their gift, say we,
   and honour
   their lore.

Today we raise one such
whose gifts are also rich
   in thought
   where scholars meet,

and where the lecture hall
invites his wit and style
   his Trinity Bay
   savvy;

whose time is never so planned
as to exclude a friend
   or stint
   a student;

and who has dear concerns
at home – a wife and bairns
   to educate
   his heart

in loyalty's costly school,
costliest school of all
   not least for
   an administrator.

The Good Book's sentiments
anent doves and serpents:
   Go forth
   as both,

gentle as one, it says,
and as the other, wise!
   words meant
   for a saint

with hair shirt and lice;
yet we expect no less
   from one
   who takes on

a university,
saintly or not saintly;
   who,
   hand to the plough,

must look wealth in the eye,
power and policy,
 not to say his own
 union;

must hold Learning dear,
critic and comforter,
 and yet draw
 a straight furrow.

May he, amid all this,
reserve leisure for tennis
 and uncluttered time
 for home.

Now is cluttered time,
yet splendid, fraught time,
ceremonious time.
Dame Ceremony, come
 and dress
 in ceremoniousness
 academically gorgeous
 these solemnities.

GEORGE'S ACROSTIC

Gods, when they give their gifts, are whimsical.
Easy to make a man knowledgeable,
or so they seem to feel, but then they grow
righteous, and make him think as well as know.
Gruesome combination, knowledge and thought:
every god knows as much, if not he ought.

Whether gifts or not, they are not given free;
hard work they cost, neglect, uncertainty,
anguish of worshipping Perfection's face
lo, in her unattainable far place,
lovely, alluring, and beyond embrace.
Elegance be her surrogate the while:
yearn as we do, make elegant our style.

Pleasure it is, though fleeting, to write well,
oil of midnight to burn, and so excel;
Eloquence, that unruly steed, to curb,
teach him the manners of the noun and verb.

Art, artifice, every device of art,
new, old, timeless, whatever speak its part
deliberately, with elegance, from the heart.

Sit in the sun, loaf and invite the soul?
Come, never let Oblivion cajole!
Hold for Perfection's unattained aureole.
Owls are her birds, they blink and blink at us.
Let them not blink equivocally thus!
All be our way but faith, our hope good will,
rue nothing, sharpen pens, write still, write still!

FIN DE TOUR WITH SUSAN AND BILL

Agin the first light come, on again
on again, on the train,
half awake, breakfasted,
bill's rhythms on the brain
sovereign against the pain.
Onward the Council bears
us, first class, no less,
onward to British ears
eager to hear us three
make with our poetry.
Night light, read again,
me first, Susan then
raises that dancing man
Harry; bill's turn
turns loos th yunicorn.
'Honey' winds up the fun.
First light, on again
on again and on again.
Too bad, soon it ends.
Ah, then goodbye good friends.
What eye will then be dry?
Susan will shed a tear,
bill too, me too,
tears, tears everywhere.
So long, dancing man,
so long, unicorn
till we meet again.

A RETURN FOR GEORGE BOWERING

New-fangled, old-fangled,
in, either way;
craftily wit-spangled
eulogy. I may say

praise from a younger poet,
offered so freely,
elates me, as you know it
must. It seems hardly

yesterday I was young, but not so
outgoing, more willing to
underpraise my elders than you.

Wisdom is said to come with age.
Right: I seem to have grown
old enough and sage
to catch a bouquet thrown,
especially such a fine one.

Acrostic is always a lark,
but in an upside-down sonnet,
only you would embark
unabashedly on it,
tickled when you had done it.

Masterful in its apparent
ease of clear statement.

Graceful too, since you speak of grace:
end-rhymed gracefully;
orderly in form and pace;
reasonable, as it should be.
Gifts ask a return in kind:
Ever yours gratefully, George, signed
                          GJ

A MARRIAGE POEM FOR PEG AND JOHN

Word from oversea,
  happy word
  finds its way
round Earth's round by chancy
  post and telephone
  making Peg's and John's
  decision
  known.

What but wed
ought people do?
  Once decided
  it seems obvious.
Mark always knew,
  but not us,
  we did not know
  until the gleeful
  transAtlantic
word came through.

Married life is what
one makes it; there is luck,
  blissful times – and not,
  thin and thick,
  just sitting it out;
  all part of the life.
May you make the lot.

May Content alight,
   that sly comer
   whose look bemuses pain;
may he preen his wing
and sing
and sing again,
   and as the years narrow
   against oncoming night,
his golden, late note.

A SPRING EVENING WALK WITH LUKE

Strapped on
head under my chin
asleep, your noises
echo cries
a few late birds
utter into nightfall;
other only
sound, wind
that gusts cold from the west.

Sun's red
lowered into then
leaves behind overcast
now.

I hold your head
and its archaic dream
long since drowned in mine.
Your squeaks
and clucks
and my footfall
sound our note in the dusk.

A MARRIAGE POEM FOR NORA AND JAMIE

North comes the sun for summer
               a sending forth
of jubilant flame; he rays out
               in regal splendour
nor is it a little he shines on
               sweetly,
on all our faces at this wholly
               new age-old event,
just the same event that Adam
               and Eve
in new-formed innocence adorned
               dear originals,
joining in amiable bands
               yet blessed hands.
News, at the Border another
               knitting together;
again, the genial game between
               genders
played not for a paltry stake but restored
               paradise
no less. Imagine aiming so high! truly
               young Amity
need only shore against
               his own too much,
his generous fame and equally
               gentle name.
Genius of the day, may he
               delaying not
now pour a full blessing
               on our pair
their nuptial joys well begun, Jamie and Nora made one.

SEAMUS'S ACROSTIC

Sure the same genius
               that smiles on his parents
eyes their issue with favour
               as everyone must,
also shapes his omens
               us to make glad,
marshalling his main
               and magnanimous
utmost: shade of his arm
               over him, trustworthy,
Seamus, new son,
               scion of Quinn.

Ask Again   Part Two: 'Marriages, Births, Deaths'

KATY

One
day old

asleep
in her mother's arms

whose labour
past

smiles
in the doorway.

Her new babe.

MAGGIE'S ACROSTIC

Mild-mannered girl,
               much given to smile,
amiable, ongoing,
               ingrained with glee,
glad-magic gowned,
               green-hearted, her
growth matches grace,
               golden lass to be;
imitates anger
               ably, not grieves,
every inch Maggie,
               eternal she.

LAURA'S FUNERAL

Much gets remembered: the good
she did; how she did it,
as though, What else but do good?
Small things too, the tilt
of her gait and smile,
a way she had of turning up
without warning.
That was her way of going.

At her funeral
it welled up and brimmed over.
Then her priest tells a story
that brings back
her all but presence.

A life takes on its meaning
at the end, however sad,
however unbearable.
Dear God, dear dead, it gets borne.

REMEMBERING BETTY

Oncoming winter's dark and cold;
you felt come the time
tells Time self told:
said to the time, Come,
    when is now.

Deliberately, with strict forethought and care,
hour and means your own,
chose everywhere and nowhere
and there went, alone,
    knowing.

Who guessed at conclusions infinite pursued
resolving to such now
at the far brink of good,
last gather of how,
    music's close?

Holed for breath, your words came halt.
Your words yet, as before;
no word of ill you felt
or how your patience wore
    year by year

opened, pain and death standing by,
closed and home again,
wit still bright in your eye,
beauty bright in your mien
    after

drugs, diagnostics, probings, the worry
of healing's learned chase,
you being not quarry,
quarry's lurking place
    covert and prey.

There was never illness in your life's kindness
nor ever in your heart's elegance
nor bitterness
of your heart's blood's mischance
    ever.

ELEGY FOR GEORGE WHALLEY

Dear George, a tardy goodbye;
early your twilight ended;
after what seemed a solemn
reprieve – summoned again.

Go, I thought then, however
eternity takes you. So
outwit patching and wasting.
Regret nothing unfinished;
give others leave to finish;
empty your head of it. Go.

Writing now, I am mindful
how easy it was to think.
Arrived at that shore, whose eye
looks calmly forth, whose courage
launches boldly on that deep?
Even your forward spirit
yearned back to Earth at the last.

Pain, weakness, then restlessness,
oxygen hunger, gasping,
evils of a long illness,
tried the pitch of your music

so high, we tremble to think.
Children live close to death.
Heart ages, grows vulnerable
over a lifetime of love,
loss, lookings-about in fear
as though to muster forces,
rear-guard *perdus* against the world.

Does your courtesy, that seemed
endless, impregnable, your
antique chivalry live on,
renew affections in us?

For us your poetry and prose
remain; we see them as though
incised in ivory, precise,
enduring, light in darkness;
nobility of phrase that
discerns light from our darkness.

Hard to imagine now your
absence, your smile no longer
inviting, your friendliness,
learning, to know they are gone.

All changes, though there is no
new thing, only what is old
driving on, altering, and on.

Fingers of the disease wrought
artistry of your deep
resources, made you ghostly,
exquisite, still the same hid
wistfulness always in your
eyes, inward of the way you
looked out from your bridge. That
lingers....

LESSON ONE

Do not give up your bees
now, Fred, after all these
years learning their thunder.
You should apprentice me.
See if I cant be taught.
So I say in the heat
of the hayfield; hiveward
nectar and pollen draw
bee-lines by our heads. Well,
says Fred, I plan to take
honey off tomorrow.
I got an extry veil.
Offer is one thing, make
up my mind another.
But I agree. Why not?
As the old saying says,
Jump first and then swither.
Bee-weather next forenoon;
cloudless, a benign sun.
I am veiled and assigned
the mystery of smoke;
not adequately gloved,
however, as I find
before the day has lived
itself much older. Awk,
poof, you make a man choke
with that smoker! I know.
I am amazed by so
many bees in the world.

Why ever would someone
have thought out all these bees?
Mind putting that super
back on top over there?
we'll take it off next time,
it's full of brood. I up
it in place with a plop.
Stings between glove and sleeve
shove themselves in my wrist;
Earth's many-pronged foretaste.
Fred is getting it too.
Bees dont like to be jarred.
Lesson one, a hard one:
go gently; likewise get
proper gloves; likewise let
not your hand be hurried
by numbers in the world.

FIREFLY EVENING

Heft of earth, under;
evening's heft, thunder;
evening of fireflies;
thunder in western skies.

Airs through windows yet
and through the downstairs let
that over pastures come
thunder from.

ECSTATIC

When basswood blows   bees make in it,
mill in midsummer   myriad pillage;
probing to pull out   pollen and sweetness
they swing sure-foot   searching of mouth.
A massive murmur   moves through the basswood
and breathes blissful   her bosom kiss.
Caressed queen   she crowns the season,
her senses swarming   in shared ferment.

BOON

Heat-weary head   the humid morning
moves with mounting   menace into day;
dims the deep woods,   dulls the skyline.
Sullen, slow-paced   sisterhood of haze
hover hang-breasted   hairy over fields,
fill with forthcoming   flood and thunder.
Thirst threads earth   in thin rootlets,
reaches restlessly   rock-branched for water
waiting for weather's   wild-handed boon.
Breath, a first breeze   brightens aspens
airy, easy.   All at once dark
dour-faced, driving,   day's burden
bursts in a blind flash   blunders among trees,
twists over tops,   tears bits away.
Outgush, Earth-hammer   issue of gods,
grandeur that gives   and grieves, magnificent.

EASTWARD

Trod-on Earth   turn for us
anxious ones   into dusk,
deepen into   dark kindly,
clearing off   cloud vestiges,
vapour trails   that vex heaven,
had purposes   hoving westward.

Wake eastward: wide-face moon
emerge.

THE RINGERIKE STYLE

Where, in the north half-world,
Viking farmer tilled
or beached on a far shore
he left his runic mark
on stone, bronze, horn
or wood: thin-chiselled
bird, beast, flower,
interlaced and scrolled.

A lengthened-out dragon,
lion or chimerical
lengthened-out creature
swallows its own tail
or another creature's tail,
all the lengthening-out
a flat lattice work
of interlocked length.

A boulder with a snake
of runes cut in it
remembers a helmeted man
in a long ship: *At Holmgard*
he fell, the ship's captain,
with his crew. I Toste,
his son, raised this stone.

ONSET

A between time; what's to come
looms. Let it not loom.
It has loomed enough.
Let it, whatever it is, loom off.

Bang go hunters in the woods, the woods
light up: amber, ochre, crimson. Bang,
more colour; along
the She-Woods Road amber clerestories.
Them hunters, it aint safe. Bang
bang bang go end of summer flies
in the lampshades, bang around the room
dying lazy. Eva dies at last.
We're makin out ok since the wife passed on.
Them two years gone, eh? Nothin but care.
Done with, now.
Eva.
Given back.

End of summer chime
in the aftergrass, did did, did did,
almost done. Overhead
looms the redtail
for the little ones
his circles as near
perfect as the lazy
season makes them,
his plunge
the plunge.

Moonrise
over Kelsey's apple trees
blazons winter's onset.

SWEPT SKY

Titanic fall of the year,
passion of savage splendour
loosed by the gale, blowing bare

in gusts that comb high colour
bronze by bronze, crimson by reft
crimson. It is the dolour

of passage that I feel, my
helplessness. I am helpless
as leaves under the swept sky.

      * * *

I imagine myself not
whimpering, stoic, enduring
I cannot imagine what.

But today I am not sure;
cries are carried on the wind
from my fellows everywhere

and I hear them as my own,
my voice crying through the trees
and with the coloured leaves blown.

      * * *

Above the unrest a great
passenger aircraft bellows
lofting its cargo of fate

on its fire-erupting storm
and hazard of circuitry.
I walk briskly to keep warm

and am in hazard too, not
aloft but wind-buffeted,
mindful of my earth-bound lot.

WHITE

Dream, she says,
drawing her drifts about her,
when you lie broken
on the road
or wherever you get broken,
my cold in your breaks,
dream
of my white.

Or in another mood,
come
unbroken
into my inward,
sun burning through,
enter my forest of frost feathers.

Orange for berries.
Red, black, ochre and straw-coloured hairs,
black limbs, black trunks,
her beech leaves russet,
evergreens burdened;

and what she does with her fingers.

Know what she means,
then come.

FROST

Frost on my window;
night comes creaking up

close.
Stars crowd.

LET GO

Midst of mid-winter white-limbed woods
brook makes his icy coax
where my footfall intrudes:
Come to my icy rocks,
    blinding waters.

Earth's over again over again theme,
chanted in her brooky throat:
Come, little one, come home.
I meditate her note:
    Ever, never.

Road makes its way downhill and again uphill
twice, at the brook and at a gully.
It has a story to tell
I follow only fitfully
    more aware

of small goings-on among the trees and undergrowth,
purposes my presence modifies
briefly, of snout and tooth
and bill. Some I recognize,
    some I do not.

Trees tick and let drop snow
that falls in veils among their ranks.
An air in the stillness and they let go,
or an impulse deep in their trunks
    I feel in mine.

COME THROUGH

Day after day wet
sky, wet snow, earth
earthiness
under.

Knows
to come through:
drink
snow.

Stubble first, then
ploughland,
lumpy terrain,
mud.

All the while brook
takes his walk
woodlot to woodlot
talking
among his alders.

SPRING CHORUS

Spring keeps coming in louder
in Fred's
moonwet
gravel pit:

be glad
squeeze me
o be gladder
o squeeze squeeze
o squeeze

not

says no
says claw
in the wet
move over
splash
hush

again
maybe a little
squeeze again
glad maybe
o squeeze o be gladder
o squeeze squeeze
squeeze

TENTATIVE

May, a first pair
of swallows, in and out
the barn window;
soon air
will thrive
with their concerns
but now
these two,
tentative
of all returns.

MAJESTIC

Cats catch birds, birds
fly after crows, a king–
bird will chase a big
hawk, make her dodge,
hurry to the woods.

Three herons have been seen twice
flying in a ring.

Heron stalks
frog
or fish
then lifts and oars off.

Majestic.

A TOAST TO WILLIAM MORRIS

for his 155th birthday party,
given by The William Morris Society of Canada

Gather us erring folk, Master Morris,
Unto your myth, realm of your inmost thought:
Knights and ladies in seductive chorus,
Sigurd, Brynhild, Guenore and Lancelot,
Heroes and gods and powers that they ought,
In proper rhymes and metres, as of old;
How better may such lofty things be told?

What better language? ay, and in good sooth:
No common archaisms, but your own,
In which to clothe your vision of the truth,
Your hopes for humankind, though heedless grown;
So clear a vision and so sweet a tone;
A sad tone too, for things that might have been
And might yet be, but that greed falls between.

Happiness was your generous, true note:
A life of happy work for everyone;
Yet there were many tears in what you wrote,
For pride of workmanship, by trade undone,
Indeed, for how your own life's love had gone;
Angry tears for neglect of human worth,
And brute callousness of the lords of Earth.

What news would you bring back from Nowhere now
If you could share with us our mortal stay?
What dream would be provoked by our knowhow,
Our breakthrough, megadeath, our day-by-day,
The revolution having made its way
Through suffering that you did almost guess
Lurks in brave plans for common happiness?

You did not fathom our depravity,
Our willingness to squander and destroy;
Yet we must bless you for your charity
And glad example of your craftsman's joy
That kept at bay for you life's deep annoy,
Or seemed to do – what can we ever know?
You said, Love is enough. We take you so.

MARGARET LAURENCE 1926-1987

Tell no longer
stories of our women,
how they make with their men,
their young, their selves.

Lived in them,
spoke through them
and for them

as she spoke for us.
Our sister, Margaret,
spared herself nothing.
Was spared old age.

Later Poems

a dedicatory poem

Where in the wide world not?
What opera not attended
once, twice, three times?
What book not read?
What wise thought not thought
and wisely written
with keeping and wit?
And that is not all: teaching –
teacher of heart and eye
and ear,
inward of teaching, inward of poetry,
friend of poets;
friend of good fellowship, good talk
good stories,
and after a blessed fast
joyous feasting.

Laborare est orare:
God's patient scribe
and bedesman,
our Bill, our WFB,
Professor Blissett.

A RETIREMENT PARTY POEM FOR GORDON WOOD

Out of the west, i.e. Weston
    up to Toronto the good,
his freshman tie and the rest on
    comes young Lochinvar Wood,

on the old Ontario Strand
    among God-fearing youth
to take the World in hand
    and free it by means of the Truth.

A naughty world it was
    that marched us all off to war.
Who could resist the Great Cause?
    Not he, not Wood Lochinvar.

Square-bashing invaded his days,
    combat training, parades, marches past;
then rumours of postings, delays,
    and King George's troopship at last.

Air-bombed in the Med, the ship sinks;
    Wood swims to the African shore.
Re-grouped with his Irish, he thinks,
    What a wet introduction to war!

When ladies of Italy spied
    this gallant young officer lad,
Bambino, bambino! they cried;
    so young and so handsome! How sad!

But sad he was not, he was scared
    and courageous, patrolling by night,
attacking by day. He was spared
    to come home and look back on the fight.

George paid him to study again.
    He was brilliant, he shone like a star,
reading Edmund and Will and rare Ben
    and the Countess of Feuillerat's Ar-

kidney; tome after tome
    until it came out at his ears.
Then off to make Carleton his home:
    our Gordon to be, all these years.

What did we not teach from our small
    First Avenue quarters of yore,
desks cluttered, books high on the wall,
    and Chairman Munro next door?

Woody you were, the scribe
    of the Engineers' rude reviews.
When Hilda entertained the tribe
    you buttled the cakes and the booze.

Now you are one of the seniors.
    What next? What indeed but the sky?
A colourful life has been yours.
    Old soldiers, they say, never die,

they just fade away, somehow.
    No hurry, leave timing to fate.
Enjoy what is left of the now.
    We shall watch for you at the gate.

FOR PEYTON LYON'S RETIREMENT PARTY
DECEMBER 4, 1988

Off the African shore
   we escorted convoys
huddling north to the War
   with men, guns and supplies,

we four in an armed room
   of air-sustained metal,
half the round Earth from home;
   watchdogs of sea battle.

You, our navigator,
   dead reckoned all the way
with pencil, mercator,
   compass and plain savvy.

Wide-ocean rendezvous,
   you took us there and back,
and what you always knew
   was where and when on track.

Homewards across the coast
   exactly when and where,
hungry and tempest tossed
   with petrol just to spare.

Comradeship of that war
   has held together since,
paths crossing near and far,
   lean years and affluence.

Now we are homing again
   towards another coast
not knowing where or when
   this landfall may be crossed.
   God's good time for a feast.

A PALIMPSEST FOR JOHN NEWLOVE'S
FIFTIETH BIRTHDAY PARTY

Everyone is wise. John Newlove is
   a master in his versifying and he
knows things he cannot explain to the others,
   though he tries as hard as he can anyways.

God only knows what he is up to tonight
   making his way to eternity, through destiny
manufacturing chaos into rhythms
   and all the while observing himself

wrapped for fifty years in the cold dark cloak
   of fate, and making poetry of his doubts.
How splendid, how pregnant, all his poetry,
   and not composed of vegetable peels, either.

How important it makes him in our eyes.
   Though we are in a land of loonies, we can feel
that he has done us all good in his fifty years
   and we hope he will have many more to do us good.

It has been a long, dear association
   making the alien recognizable
in ourselves – and why should it ever end?
   Think of that, John, if you can bear it, tonight.

FOR ROBIN'S SIXTIETH BIRTHDAY

When I get to Heaven
whom shall I say I know?

Robin Skelton,
wizard of the measured line.

Under a big hat
among whiskers

someone wise
and generous.

Skelton? Ah, yes.
But does he know you?

I preen myself
and smile.

CROWS' NESTS IN COURT METRES

for PK, in admiration for her 'Crows' Nests'

Gisli's tale beguiles you:
gold-breaker, bold smiter,
hard-pressed poet outlaw,
prince of artificers;
rhymed he in wrought metres
ruefully, his broodings
dreams of deep-browed women,
dark and bright harbingers.

Clear are your uncluttered
cadences, that radiate
brave wit and bright, ringing
bell notes; now they welcome
norse metric; new-turned it
knows you for its poet,
skilful in your scaldic
version, Page excursion.

Crows' nests in court metres
call forth your resources:
outlandish, extravagant
images, one simply
marvels at your merry
music; your abusive
sharpwitted, showering
showdown with black crowdom.

Later Poems

I do not remember names.

You say your name is Mephisto
Pheles. Pheles your last name?

Do I know you from somewhere?

     * * *

Why should I want to be happier?
says the Accuser
who inhabits the unhappy.

     * * *

Our way home paid.

So far,
so much to pay,
such effort

to lift a floor in air
for underfoot.

     * * *

LIGHTNING

Does the tree know
its trunk full charged
and take the stroke?

YET ANOTHER SLIM VOL

Surely one of the rootedest
of our senior Canadian poets,
most ante post-post-modernist
most / least *je ne sais quoi,* as befits
this many-faceted volume
with all its felicities,
honed, every one of them,
honed is the word for these,
unless we should let, perhaps,
the serviceable word 'crafted'
fall from our critic's lips.
In what sense crafted? Well, crafted.
Anyone knows in what sense.
Savour this: 'The moonlight shafted
into the bedroom. Pots
were falling in all the kitchens.
I am heavy with heavy thoughts.'
How true a poetic stance
for these pot-falling times!
Made vivid with circumstance
and deftly archaic with rhymes.
Poetics hold no terrors
for this unbuttoned style,
these brazen syntactical errors,
that swift, inscrutable smile.

It is good to see an old veteran
still churning it out with the rest:
each slender new volume a better one
as though there could never be best;
each year after year a new insight –
insightfullest poet around;
almost best poet, if not quite –
such judgements are made in a half light,
one might go on judging the whole night,
our poets are thick on the ground.

RESTORED

Whether Lazarus
    laughed again –
Bishop Cardinal Fisher
    says not.

1509
    Duchess of Richmond's
funeral sermon:
'restored to the mysteries of this lyfe agayn
    he never laugh.'

Jesus wept
before his miracle.

PITY

Get off the road, snake,
  laze not in the sun
sunning your snake ache;
  move on, little one!

Nudging with my boot.
  Snake flickers and strikes;
thinks better of it;
  so much for me, takes

snake anger and all
  off to privity.
No rest for the small.
  Damn human pity!

PITY

Get off the road, snake,
    laze not in the sun
sunning your snake ache;
    move on, little one!

nudging with my boot.
    Snake flickers and strikes;
thinks better of it;
    so much for me; takes

snake anger and all
    off to privity.
No rest for the small.
    Damn human pity!

LIFE

Skunk shot here,
his amble brought to an end
at the foot of this old tree.

Tree, you look raggeder
than wormy skunk,

your thick branches broken
in disarray.

A hole high in your trunk
says o.

Up top in some twigs
life yet.

Life in the skunk too.

TERROR

Single-minded women,
vengeful men
with engines
of random cruelty:
their discontents
draw me.

God in heaven judge
between
their rage for childhood's
anarchy,
and the righteousness of greed
heartless for more.

CREATION

*for Gerald Trottier,
especially for his 'Easter Series' paintings*

You stand in your island studio,
a bare canvas big in front of you,
your thought big with what you mean to paint:
I blench to think what; my heart grows faint.

The thing itself, God's poor bare forked us,
creatures of God's hand, wilful, anxious,
at home and not at home anywhere
on bludgeoned earth, in envenomed air.

A while since, you painted a far green
country. Did you long for that serene?
Did you see the land of lost content,
or glimpse, perhaps, what Creation meant?

Fiat, fiat! the saint's driven cry:
you look at us as with the saint's eye,
fellow mortals in Creation's chance
the Word chose, and launched intelligence.

What courage we know we know by fear,
life by death, hope we know by despair.
Must it be so? Is our Paradise
without courage and hope, without price?

Sweet love and hate, pride and bitter fall:
what cost our Paradise, after all?
Are the losses that we suffer here
what make dear all that we hold most dear?

Grief we cannot seem to live without:
we make trouble when we have it not.
Direst horrors are those ourselves make:
are these also for Creation's sake?

John heard, Behold, I make all things new.
God with us did live our darkest through;
taught the word of love and no word wrote;
lived a book that warring sides may quote.

Children of that Life, how ought we pray?
What you paint, Gerald, is what you say,
and what you live, that too is your word:
all one word, with the Creator Word.

POEMS ABOUT THE WIND

Come, wind,
thump the house,
trouble sleep;
nights, mustering
across the fields;

days, towering
embodied
in blowing snow.

       * * *

Wind scours the fields
of snow, snow melt
pours along the ditches.

A crow fights the wind
to a topmost twig
and rocks there.

       * * *

Wind roar on my left
among the trees;

March gust
finds its voice
in branches,

roars and goes off.

SNOWFALL IN STILL WEATHER

Earlie's woods
crouch,

his fences
file across the white.

I halt
homeward,

catch flakes
on my tongue.

HASTE

September; warm; watching Antares burn
low to the trees. We are approaching him
with unimaginable haste, says one of us;
light-years haste, not to be imagined.

In star-warm dusk, watching the big star set.

Later Poems

at five weeks

A thousand air miles
into the North woods
to see your first smiles,
hardly there and gone,
sweetly there again.

Little new begun
smile, as the year's fall
colours the shore trees.
Loon calls from your lake
her summer's end call,
readying coastwards,
her fledglings too;
night rings with their cries.
Now the winter stars,
Taurus, Orion,
Dog and Pleiades
begin their slow climb.
See, they shine for you.

LAURA & JOHN OLAF

David and Cathleen
have a blue-eyed daughter
whom they name Laura Jeanne,
Jeanne for her grandmother.

Smiling, blue-eyed lass,
old a quarter year,
smiles, and her eyes cross
at her big brother

two-year-old John Olaf,
he who wonders can,
who can make her laugh,
cry, sometimes,
make her laugh again.

SOLOMON'S ACROSTIC

Shot with Sibylline shows Everywhere
opens her Everything, item by item,
lays bare her liveliest loveliness, innocent
only as you are, age eighteen months;
marvelling man-child, moving outward.
Outward is all now, inward comes later;
now all is Nature's new-bright event.

JONATHAN

At midnight comes your knock.
Full summer, full moon, full term for you.
Water, blood, your first light
emerging.

Three hours in air
asleep,
your angels and their giant sons asleep,
and your Noah.

What shall we say?
Pop a cork at the ceiling,
drink to your name
Jonathan

and marvel.
Here you are.
When again will your mere
being be so much?

JOHN OLAF

Waited for you, John Olaf;
you came in your own
appointed time
head first

from all-knowing
into our wonderment.
As you grow we grow
to meet you

until you make us your own.
What then?
You grin
and wag feet and fists.

We are your fate now, John Olaf,
us you must dree;
and our loves that are veined
with awe.

A MARRIAGE POEM FOR BOB AND LAUREL

Back for a new life
in the old North;
city din adieu,
come wilderness voices
and silences.

What but a good life there
we look for and wish for you
together; your both voices
and dear silences.

Between city and wild
many in-betweens;
good friends in all
to breakfast and feast with.

May you venture worldwards
somewhiles, among us;
northwards too, when the notion
takes you, into the scrub;
but find your contentments
homewards, wherever.

OLD TUNE

A tune my mother sang
   in my head
sings to my sleeping
   childhood.

All day
   one tune,
earliest yearnings
   in it.

The Lay of Thrym

INTRODUCTION

'The Lay of Thrym' was probably first heard in the hall of a Norse
prince or chieftain some time during the Viking Age, perhaps as early
as the ninth century. It was one of many such lays about gods and
heroes that were common among the Germanic peoples of Northern
Europe. Such Old English poems as *Beowulf* and *Deor* draw on the
same sources. Few have survived and almost all of these few,
including 'The Lay of Thrym', are to be found in the most famous of
the Icelandic manuscript codices, now known as the *Codex Regius of
the Poetic Edda* (GKS 2365 4to), dated to the second half of the
thirteenth century. It came into the hands of Bishop Brynjólf of
Skálholt in the seventeenth century. He presented it, along with other
Icelandic manuscripts, to King Frederick III of Denmark, and it
remained in the Royal Danish Library until it was recently returned to
Iceland, first of the many Icelandic manuscripts to come back from
Denmark, where they had been carefully preserved. These are now
housed and cared for in the Arnamagnaean Institute in Reykjavík.

The poems in the *Codex Regius* comprehend two main themes: in
the first part of the book are stories of the gods and presentations of
their wisdom and knowledge. The greatest of these is the *Völuspá* or
Sybil's Prophecy, a vision of the end of things, whose similarities to
the apocalypse of St. John suggest an at least indirect influence. The
second part contains stories of the mortal hero Sigurd and those
connected with his story. 'The Lay of Thrym' belongs to the first part.
Its comic treatment of the gods has suggested to some scholars that it
must have been composed after the conversion of Iceland to
Christianity, in the year 1000. Others question this dating, and argue
that the gods had always been regarded with a familiarity of spirit that
would feel no disrespect in such a jocular treatment. Moreover the
poem represents Thor in his traditional role as defender of the gods,
though at the same time it gives the satanic god Loki an
uncharacteristically helpful part to play. It is a good yarn, told with a
splendid briskness of style that anticipates the ballads in its repetitions

and the way its very economical narration is carried forward by means of dialogue.

The meaning of the name *Edda* is a mystery no one has solved. It appears first on the title page of Snorri's great thirteenth-century handbook of the scaldic art, which has been known since as *Snorri's Edda*, or sometimes *The Prose Edda*. Bishop Brynjólf believed that his manuscript codex contained material that Snorri had turned to for his knowledge of the old poetic lore. He attributed the authorship of his manuscript to the early Icelandic historian, Saemund the wise, an almost mythical figure of medieval Iceland, and named it *Saemund's Edda*. More recent scholarship has exploded this attribution, and the book is now known in English as *The Codex Regius of the Poetic Edda*.

The metre of *The Lay of Thrym* was named 'fornyrdislag', meaning 'metre that uses the old words'. It has four, or exceptionally five, syllables, two of them stressed, per line. The strophes consists of eight lines, paired syntactically and by alliteration, for example: 'Off to fair-faced / Freya's palace'. Alliteration of first letters falls on one or both stressed syllables of the first line of a pair, and ideally on the first stressed syllable of the second line. I have followed the metrical pattern as strictly as I found possible in Modern English, in which a mainly Germanic vocabulary is still available. Its stresses are no longer as strongly marked as they were, but an alliterative kind of metre can still be made with them.

Two well-known translations of *The Poetic Edda* are current: Lee M. Hollander, *The Poetic Edda*, with introduction and notes, second edition, revised, University of Texas Press, 1962; Paul B. Taylor and W.H. Auden, *The Elder Edda*, with introduction and notes by Peter R. Salus and Paul B. Taylor, Faber and Random House, 1967. My translation is from the text as it is given in Jón Helgason's edition of the Eddaic Poems, *Nordisk Filologi, Eddadigte* II, Copenhagen, 1964.

I am glad to thank my good friend Olafur Halldórsson for the scholarly eye and poetic ear he brought to bear on my translation of 'The Lay of Thrim'.

THE LAY OF THRYM

Wielder Thor
awoke angry
missed his hammer
mighty thunderer,
ruffled his mane
and red whiskers,
son of Earth took
to searching about.

These words uttered
Thor first speaking:
'Hark you, Loki,
hear what I say,
nowhere to see
neither on Earth
nor in high heaven;
hammer is stolen.

Off to fair-faced
Freya's palace,
these words uttered
Thor first speaking:
'Would fetch, Freya,
your feather pelt
to help me find
my hammer, stolen?'

1 Wielder Thor
  awoke angry
  missed his hammer
  mighty thunderer,
  ruffled his mane
  and red whiskers,
  son of Earth took
  to searching about.

2 These words uttered
  Thor first speaking:
  'Hark you, Loki,
  hear what I say,
  nowhere to see
  neither on Earth
  nor in high heaven;
  hammer is stolen!'

3 Off to fair-faced
  Freya's palace,
  these words uttered
  Thor first speaking:
  'Would fetch, Freya,
  your feather pelt
  to help me find
  my hammer, stolen!'

Freya spoke:

4 'Thee would I give it
  though it were gold
  or either silver
  I would give it.'

5 Off flew Loki
  – feather pelt thundered –
  out and away
  from Asgard's ramparts,
  journeyed into
  giants' domain.

6 Thrym, giant chief,
  throned on his mound,
  gold-leashed his dogs,
  grim around him,
  made even-shorn
  manes of his horses.

Thrym said:

7 'How fare Aesir,
  how fare elves?
  Why have you journeyed
  to giants' domain?'

Loki said:

'Ill fare Aesir,
elves fare ill;
hammer missing,
have you hid it?'

Thrym said:

8 'Hammer, tell Thor,
hidden have I
eight rasts deep
under dark earth;
under it stays
unless one bring me
first the fair-faced
Freya as bride.'

9 Off flew Loki
– feather pelt thundered –
journeyed out from
giants' domain
in again over
Asgard's ramparts.

Mid-burg waiting
met him there Thor,
these words he uttered
then first speaking:

10 'Message have you
to match your toil?
Tell us aloft
your tidings' burden;
seated messengers
say more than truth,
lying down messengers
lie every word.'

Loki said:

11 'Toil have I had
and tale worth telling:
your hammer Thrym holds,
high chief giant;
under earth stays
unless one bring him
first the fair-faced
Freya as bride.'

12 Forth to fair-faced
Freya, greet her;
these words uttered
Thor first speaking:
'Bind you, Freya
in bridal linen,
journey we two
to giant's domain.'

13 Angry Freya
only snorted;
Aesir trembled
all together;
broke she Brisings'
brilliant necklace:
'Man-eager would you
make me appear,
journey with you
to giants' domain!'

14 Aesir every
one to meeting,
gods and goddesses
great ones taking
weighty counsel,
worry together,
Thor, his hammer
how recover?

15 Word from Heimdal
whitest of gods,
second-sighted
seer, like the Vanir:

'Bind on Thor's brow
bridal linen!
knot great Brisings'
necklace on him.'

16 Household key-chain
hang from his belt,
in queen-clothing
clad to his shins,
breast-adorning
brooch upon him,
finest headgear
to finish off!'

17 Then shouted Thor,
thunder-voiced god:
Arrant quean-man
Aesir will call me
if I let bind
bride-linen on me!'

18 Loud spoke Loki
Laufey's son,
'Think again, Thor,
thrust down your words!
Enter will giants
Asgard's ramparts
hither, unless home
hammer is fetched.'

19 Bound then was Thor
with bridal linen,
knotted great brisings'
necklace on him,
household key-chain
hung from his belt,
clad to his shins
in queen-clothing,
breast-adorning
brooch upon him,
finest headgear
to finish off.

20 'Listen,' said Loki
Laufey's son,
'Maidservant must I
make me with you,
journey together
to giants' domain!'

21 Goats out grazing,
  grooms fetch them in,
  harnessed, hitched up
  haul Thor's wagon.
  Broke mountain tops,
  blazed over fields,
  journeyed Odin's son
  into giants' domain.

22 Charged his men, Thrym,
  chief of giants:
  'Stand up, mighty ones,
  strew the benches!
  Forth comes fair-faced
  Freya, my queen,
  Njord of Noatun's
  noble daughter.

23 Gold-horn cattle
  graze my pastures,
  black-coated oxen
  brighten my days;
  jewels, treasures
  jammed in my boxes,
  lack I only
  the lovely Freya.'

24 On to evening,
  early came guests,
  beakers of ale
  borne in for giants.
  Ate one whole ox
  and eight salmon,
  finished off dainties
  furnished for ladies,
  gulped Sif's husband
  three gallons of mead.

25 Jaw fell of Thrym,
  giants' chieftain:
  'Ever did bride
  eat more keenly?
  Bride have I not seen
  bite more hugely
  nor maid empty
  mead horns as she!'

26 Sharp-wit servant
  sat close at hand,
  able-worded
  to answer giant:
  'Fair-faced Freya
  fasted eight days,
  journey-eager
  for giants' domain.'

27 Lifted linen,
   looked for a kiss,
   blinked, rebounded
   back through the hall:
   'Fearsome, flaming
   are Freya's eyes;
   always burn they
   so awesome bright?'

28 Sharp-wit servant
   sat close at hand,
   able-worded
   to answer giant:
   'Freya wakeful,
   fair one, eight nights,
   journey-eager
   for giants' domain.'

29 In then comes Thrym's
   ugly sister,
   boldly bride-gift
   bade them give her:
   'Reach me red-gold
   rings from your arms,
   give for my gracious
   good will and love;
   love and good will
   look both for gifts.'

30 Charged his men, Thrym,
   chief of giants:
   'Bring in hammer
   bride to hallow,
   lay in her lap
   lordly Mjollnir,
   vow we together
   Var to witness.'

31 Bosom laughter
   bellowed from Thor,
   heart of iron
   hammer brandished.
   First he felled Thrym
   foremost giant,
   all his kin then
   in order laid.

32 Slew the sister,
   sullen old maid,
   bride gift gave her
   begged at table,
   stroke on the head
   instead of coin,
   blow of hammer
   for bounty of rings.

   Home came Odin's son's
   hammer again.

The Lay of Thrym

There were two races of gods, the Aesir and the Vanir. These are Icelandic plural forms of the names, and I have kept them in preference to the English plurals, which would have been Aeses and Vanes.

Thor's hammer, Mjöllnir, was an important weapon in the gods' running strife with the giants.

Freya was one of the Vanir. She was a fertility goddess, sister of the fertility god, Frey. Her feather pelt, or shape, enabled her to fly. Her necklace, which she broke in stanza 13, and Thor, nevertheless, later wore, was the famous *Brisinga men,* also mentioned in *Beowulf,* where it is called the *Brosinga men.*

The prose lines that introduce speakers are outside the metrical pattern, and may have been added when the poem was given its written form. The strophic pattern is occasionally irregular; there should be eight lines to a strophe.

Asgard was the domain of the gods. The name means 'farm of the gods'.

Thrym's mound was probably a burial mound. Kings and chieftains favoured these as eminences from which to survey their domains.

Elves were a lesser order of divine beings.

A rast was an indeterminate measure of distance, or it may have been a measure of time taken to cover a certain distance. The word is cognate with the English word 'rest'. The Norse form of the word is 'röst'. Cleasby and Vigfusson's *Icelandic-English Dictionary* (Oxford, 1957) suggests that it may represent 'a distance after which one rests.'

Heimdal was the son of Odin. He was said to be the father of the four classes of men – thralls, free men, aristocrats and kings – by four different mothers.

Laufey is only known as Loki's mother.

Sif was Thor's wife. Her name is cognate with the Old English word *sib*, still current in 'sibling' and the second syllable of 'gossip'. She was an earth-mother figure, and goddess of wedlock and kinship.

Var was a goddess mentioned in Snorri's *Edda* as one who hears oaths and the agreements undertaken between men and women.

CONTENTS

Author's Introduction

The Cruising Auk   Part One: 'The Pool'

The Cruising Auk   Part Two: 'The Cruising Auk'

Happy Enough

Taking a Grip